ESTATE PUBLICATIONS

STAFFORDSHIRE

Street maps with index
Administrative Districts
Population Gazetteer
Road Map with index
Postcodes

Street plans prepared and published by ESTATE PUBLICATIONS, Bridewell House, TENTERDEN, KENT, and based upon the ORDNANCE SURVEY mapping with the permission of the Controller of H. M. Stationery Office.

The Publishers acknowledge the co-operation of the local authorities of towns represented in this atlas.

Estate Publications 231 D   ISBN 1 84192 048 7   © Crown Copyright 398713

COUNTY RED BOOK

STAFFORDSHIRE

contains street maps for each town centre

SUPER & LOCAL RED BOOKS

are street atlases with comprehensive local coverage

BURTON UPON TRENT

including: Ashby-de-la-Zouch, Barton-under-Needwood,
Linton, Repton, Swadlincote, Tutbury etc.

STAFFORD

including: Hopton, Penkridge, Stone, Walton-on-the-Hill etc.

STOKE-ON-TRENT

including: Alsager, Audley, Biddulph, Blythe Bridge,
Kidsgrove, Madeley, Newcastle-under-Lyme etc.

CONTENTS

COUNTY ADMINISTRATIVE DISTRICTS: pages 4-5

GAZETTEER INDEX TO ROAD MAP: pages 6-7
(with populations)

COUNTY ROAD MAP: pages 8-11

TOWN CENTRE STREET MAPS:

INDEX TO STREETS: page 56

LEGEND TO STREET MAPS

One-Way Street	→	Post Office	●
Pedestrianized	▨	Public Convenience	C
Car Park	P	Place of Worship	+

Scale of street plans: 4 Inches to 1 mile (unless otherwise stated on the map).

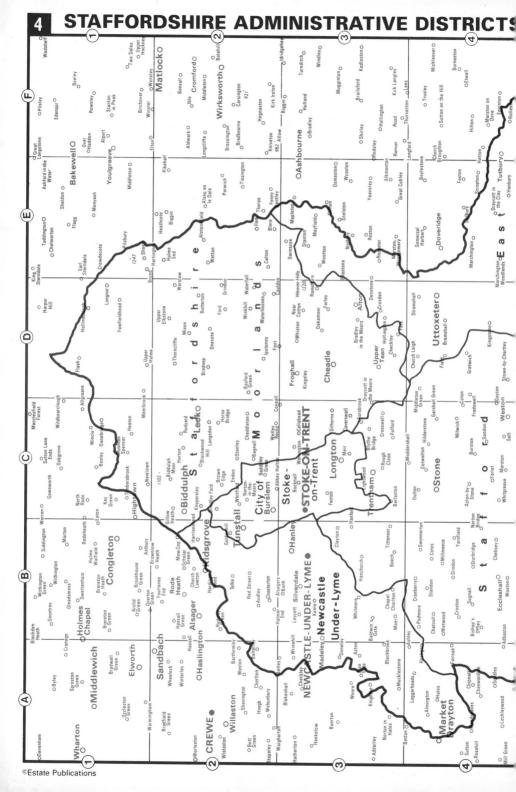

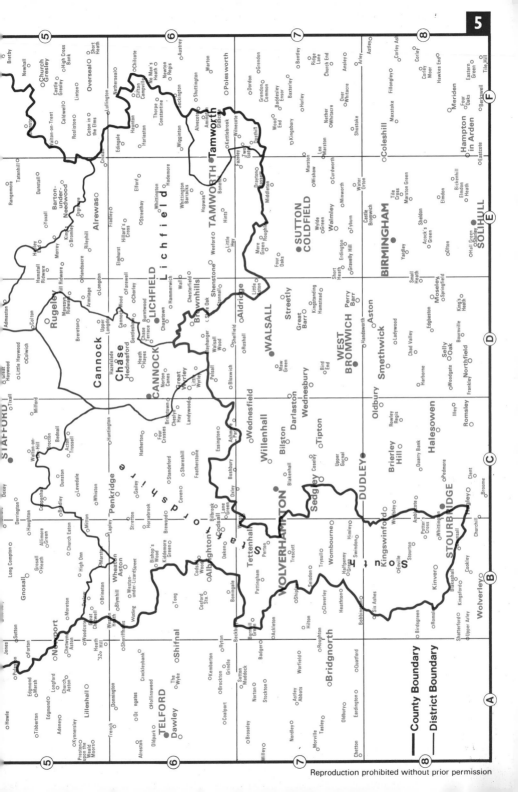

GAZETTEER INDEX TO ROAD MAPS
with Populations

County of Staffordshire population **1,031,135**

Districts:

Cannock Chase **88,833**   Stafford **117,788**
East Staffordshire **97,105**   Staffordshire Moorlands **95,450**
Lichfield **92,679**   Stoke-on-Trent **244,637**
Newcastle-under Lyme **119,091** Tamworth **70,065**
South Staffordshire **105,487**

Abbey Hulton	8 D3	Burslem	8 C3	Enville **397**	10 C5
Abbots Bromley **1,700**	9 F6	Burston & Sandon **382**	8 D6	Essington **4,750**	10 D3
Acton Trussell &		Burton-upon-Trent **47,240**	11 G1	Etchinghill	11 E1
Bednall **1,156**	10 D1	Butterton **226**	9 E3		
Adbaston **551**	8 B6			Farewell & Chorley **313**	11 F2
Admaston	11 E1	Calf Heath	10 D2	Farley **190**	9 E4
Allimore Green	10 C1	Calton	9 F3	Fawfieldhead **300**	9 E2
Almington	8 A5	Cannock **46,754**	10 D2	Fazeley **4,548**	11 G3
Alrewas **4,037**	11 F2	Cannock Wood **1,052**	11 E2	Featherstone **3,922**	10 D3
Alsagers Bank	8 B4	Castle Church **3,200**	*	Fenton **13,394**	8 C4
Alstonefield **273**	9 F3	Cauldon	9 F3	Fisherwick **174**	*
Alton **1,321**	9 F4	Caverswall **1,058**	8 D4	Flash	9 E1
Anslow **578**	9 G6	Cellahead	8 D4	Fole	9 E5
Anslow Gate	9 G6	Chapel & Hill Chorlton **341**	8 B5	Footherley	11 F3
Armitage with		Chasetown **4,273**	11 E2	Ford	9 E3
Handsacre **4,426**	11 F2	Chatcull	8 B5	Forsbrook **5,497**	8 D4
Ashley	8 B5	Cheadle **11,265**	9 E4	Forton **241**	10 B1
Aston	8 B4	Chebsey **510**	8 C6	Four Crosses	10 D2
Aston-by-Stone	8 D6	Checkley **4,328**	9 E5	Foxt	9 E4
Audley **8,358**	8 B3	Cheddleton **5,896**	8 D3	Fradley	11 F2
		Cheslyn Hay **7,015**	10 D3	Fradswell **182**	9 E6
Baddeley Green	8 D3	Chesterfield	11 F3	Froghall	9 E4
Bagnall **833**	8 D3	Chesterton	8 C3	Fulford **5,670**	8 D5
Balance Hill	9 F5	Chorley & Farewell **313**	11 F2		
Baldwin's Gate	8 B4	Church Eaton **623**	10 C1	Gailey	10 D2
Balterley **210**	8 B3	Church Leigh	9 E5	Garshall Green	8 D5
Barlaston **2,946**	8 C5	Church Mayfield	9 F4	Gayton **154**	8 D6
Barton-under-Needwood		Clayton	8 C4	Gentleshaw	11 E2
4.664	11 G1	Clifton Campville **695**	11 H2	Gillow Heath	8 C2
Basford Green	9 E3	Codsall **7,854**	10 C3	Glascote	11 G3
Bednall &		Codsall Wood	10 C3	Gnosall **5,026**	10 C1
Acton Trussel **1,156**	10 D1	Coldmeece	8 C5	Gnosall Heath	10 C1
Beech	8 C5	Colton **713**	11 E1	Goldenhill	8 C3
Berkswich **1,938**	*	Colwich **4,749**	11 E1	Gratwich	9 E6
Betley **1,000**	8 B3	Consall **150**	8 D4	Great Bridgeford	8 C6
Biddulph **19,237**	8 C2	Cookshill	8 D4	Great Chatwell	10 B2
Biddulph Moor	8 D2	Coppenhall **218**	10 C1	Great Haywood	11 E1
Bilbrook **4,991**	10 C3	Cotes	8 C5	Great Wyrley **11,002**	11 E3
Birchall	9 E3	Coton & Hopton **1,854**	8 D6	Grindon **242**	9 F3
Bishop's Offley	8 B6	Coton Clanford	10 C1		
Bishop's Wood	10 C2	Cotton **354**	9 E4	Hadley End	11 F1
Blackbrook	8 B5	Cotwalton	8 D5	Hademore	11 G2
Blackwood Hill	8 D3	Coven	10 C3	Hales	8 A5
Blithbury	10 E1	Crackley	8 C3	Halfpenny Green	10 C5
Blithfield **235**	*	Cranberry	8 B5	Halmer End	8 B3
Blore with Swinscoe **122**	9 F3	Cresswell **1,239**	8 D5	Hammerwich **4,201**	11 E3
Blymhill & Weston-under-		Croxall	11 G2	Hamstall Ridware **289**	11 F1
Lizard **581**	10 B2	Croxden **220**	9 E5	Hanbury **556**	9 G6
Blythe Bridge	8 D5	Croxton	8 B6	Hanbury Woodend	9 G6
Bobbington **535**	10 B5	Curborough & Elmhurst **172**	11 F2	Hanchurch	8 C4
Bonehill	11 G3			Handsacre with	
Bradley **396**	10 C1	Denstone **899**	9 F4	Armitage **4,426**	11 F2
Bradley in the Moors	9 E4	Derrington	10 C1	Hanford	8 C4
Bradnop **319**	9 E3	Dilhorne **519**	8 D4	Hanley	8 C4
Bradwell	8 C3	Dosthill	11 G4	Harlaston **318**	11 G2
Bramshall	9 E5	Doxey	10 D1	Harriseahead	8 C3
Branston **3,384**	11 G1	Draycott in the Clay **829**	9 G6	Hartshill	8 C4
Brereton &		Draycott in the Moors **1,151**	8 D4	Hatherton **584**	10 D2
Ravenhill **6,461**	11 E1	Drayton Bassett **820**	11 G3	Haughton **1,010**	10 C1
Brewood **7,151**	10 C2	Drointon	9 E6	Haunton	11 G2
Bridgtown **628**	10 D2	Dunstall **234**	11 G1	Hazelslade	11 E2
Brindley Ford	8 C3	Dunston **229**	10 D1	Heath Hayes &	
Brindley Heath **936**	*			Wimblebury **9,410**	11 E2
Brineton	10 B2	Eccleshall **4,606**	8 B6	Heathylee **259**	*
Brocton **1,044**	10 D1	Edingale **547**	11 G2	Heaton **286**	8 D2
Brookhouse	9 E4	Elford **549**	11 G2	Hednesford	11 E2
Brown Edge **2,539**	8 C3	Ellastone **287**	9 F4	High Offley **872**	8 B6
Brund	9 F2	Ellenhall **109**	8 C6	High Onn	10 C1
Bucknull	8 D4	Elmhurst & Curborough **172**	11 F2	Hilderstone **409**	8 D5
Burntwood **25,617**	11 E2	Endon & Stanley **3,397**	8 D3	Hillard's Cross	11 F2

6

Place	Ref	Place	Ref	Place	Ref
Hill Ridware	11 F1	Millmeece	8 C5	Stourton	10 C5
Hilton **279**	*	Milton	8 D3	Stowe-by-Chartley **1,688**	9 E6
Himley **946**	10 C5	Milwich **433**	8 D5	Stramshall	9 E5
Hints **319**	11 F3	Mitton	10 C2	Streethay **372**	11 F2
Hixon	9 E6	Mixon	9 E2	Stretton **7,432**	9 G6
Hoar Cross **196**	11 F1	Mobberley	9 E4	Stretton & Lapley **2,781**	10 C2
Hockley	11 G3	Moddershall	8 D5	Sugnall	8 B6
Hollington	9 E5	Moreton	10 B1	Sturbridge	8 C6
Hollinsclough **165**	9 E1	Morrey	11 F1	Sutton	10 B1
Hookgate	8 B5	Moss Pit	10 D1	Swindon **1,360**	10 C5
Hopton & Coton **1,854**	8 D6	Mucklestone	8 A5	Swinfen & Packington **479**	*
Hopwas	11 G3			Swinscoe with Blore **122**	9 F4
Horninglow **5,990**	9 G6	Newborough **382**	9 F6	Swynnerton **4,208**	8 C5
Horse Bridge	8 D3	Newcastle-under-			
Horsebrook	10 C2	Lyme **73,872**	8 C4	Talke **4,447**	8 C3
Horton **733**	8 D2	Newchapel	8 C3	Tamworth **70,065**	11 G3
Hulme End	9 F2	New Church	11 F1	Tatenhill **550**	11 G1
Huntington **2,892**	10 D2	Newton	9 E6	Teddesley Hay **76**	*
		Newtown	8 D2	Thorncliffe	9 E2
Ilam **127**	9 F3	Norbury **310**	10 B1	Thorpe Constantine **101**	11 G2
Ingestre **127**	8 D6	Norton Bridge	8 C6	Tittensor	8 C5
Ipstone **1,422**	9 E3	Norton Canes **6,549**	11 E2	Tittesworth **301**	*
		Norton East	10 E2	Tixall **196**	10 D1
Keele **1,203**	8 B4	Norton in the Moors	8 C3	Trentham **15,588**	8 C4
Kettlebrook	11 G3			Trescott	10 C4
Kiddemore Green	10 C3	Oakamoor **663**	9 E4	Trysull & Seisdon **1,095**	10 C4
Kidsgrove **24,132**	8 C3	Oaken	10 C3	Tunstall **11,283**	8 C3
King's Bromley **1,076**	11 F1	Okeover **76**	*	Tutbury **3,249**	9 G6
Kingsley **2,336**	9 E4	Onecote **241**	9 E3	Two Gates	11 G3
Kingsley Holt	9 E4	Onneley	8 B4		
Kingstone **614**	9 E6	Orgreave	11 F1	Upper Elkstone	9 E2
Kinver **6,748**	10 C5	Orslow	10 B2	Upper Hulme	9 E2
Knighton	8 A5	Oulton	8 D5	Upper Longdon	11 E2
Knighton	8 B6	Outwood **1,889**	*	Upper Tean	9 E5
Knypersley	8 C3			Uttoxeter **10,329**	9 E5
		Pattingham &		Uttoxeter Rural **1,378**	*
Landywood	10 D3	Patshull **2,283**	10 C4		
Lane Green	10 C3	Penkridge **8,565**	10 D2	Wall **448**	11 F3
Lapley & Stretton **2,781**	10 C2	Perton **11,336**	10 C4	Walton-on-the-Hill	10 D1
Lawnhead	8 C6	Podmore	8 B5	Warslow & Elkstones **310**	9 E2
Leek **19,850**	8 D3			Waterfall	9 F3
Leekfrith **362**	*	Quarnford **230**	*	Waterhouses **1,060**	9 E3
Leigh **806**	*			Weeford **192**	11 F3
Levedale	10 D1	Ramshorn **17**	9 F4	Weeping Cross	10 D1
Leycett	8 B4	Rangemore	11 G1	Wergs	10 C3
Leyfields	11 G3	Ranton **415**	10 C1	Werrington **6,100**	8 D4
Lichfield **28,666**	11 F2	Red Street	8 C3	Westlands	8 C4
Lightwood	8 D4	Rileyhill	11 F2	Weston **677**	8 D6
Little Aston **2,566**	11 F3	Rocester **1,432**	9 F5	Weston Coyney	8 D4
Little Hay	11 F3	Rolleston on Dove **3,203**	9 G6	Weston Jones	10 B1
Little Haywood	11 E1	Rough Close	8 D5	Weston-under-Lizard	
Little Stoke	8 D5	Rudyard	8 D2	& Blymhill **581**	10 B2
Little Wyrley	11 E3	Rugeley **17,043**	11 E1	Wetley Rocks	8 D3
Littleworth	11 E2	Rushton Spencer **444**	8 D2	Wetton **155**	9 F3
Loggerheads **4,355**	8 A5			Wetwood	8 B5
Long Compton	10 C1	Salt & Enson **438**	8 D6	Wheaton Aston	10 C2
Longdon **1,542**	11 F2	Sandon & Burston **382**	8 D6	Whiston	9 E4
Longdon Green	11 F2	Saredon **693**	*	Whiston	10 C2
Longnor **392**	9 F2	Seighford **2,483**	8 C6	Whitgreave **155**	8 C6
Longsdon **563**	8 D3	Seisdon & Trysull **1,095**	10 C4	Whitmore **1,274**	8 C5
Longton **12,860**	8 C4	Shallowford	8 C6	Whittington	10 C6
Lower Penn **1,639**	10 C4	Shareshill **698**	10 D3	Whittington **3,188**	11 F2
		Shebdon	8 B6	Wiggington **996**	11 G3
Madeley **3,796**	8 B4	Sheen **234**	9 F2	Wildwood	10 D1
Madeley Heath	8 B4	Shenstone **6,890**	11 F3	Winkhill	9 E3
Maer **550**	8 B5	Silverdale **7,124**	8 B4	Winshill **6,746**	11 H1
Marchington **1,253**	9 F6	Six Ashes	10 B5	Wombourne **13,711**	10 C4
Marchington Woodlands	9 F6	Slindon	8 C5	Woodseaves	8 B6
Marston **152**	10 C2	Stafford **53,079**	10 D1	Wootton	8 C6
Marston	8 D6	Standeford	10 D3	Wootton **134**	9 F4
Mavesyn Ridware **991**	11 E1	Standon **776**	8 C5	Wrinehill	8 B4
May Bank	8 C4	Stanley & Endon **3,397**	8 D3	Wychnor **75**	*
Mayfield **1,260**	9 F4	Stanton **202**	9 F4		
Meerbrook	98D2	Stockton Brook	8 D3	Yarlet	8 D6
Meir **14,413**	8 D4	Stoke on Trent **177,099**	8 C4	Yarnfield	8 C5
Meir Heath	8 D5	Stone **12,645**	8 D5	Yoxall **1,802**	11 F1
Middleton Green	8 D5	Stone Rural **2,295**	*		
Milford	10 D1	Stonnall **1,636**	11 F3		

Population figures are based upon the 1991 census and relate to the local authority area or parish as constituted at that date. Boundaries of the districts are shown on pages 4-5. Places with no population figure form part of a larger local authority area or parish.

Population figures in bold type.

*Place not included on map due to limitation of space

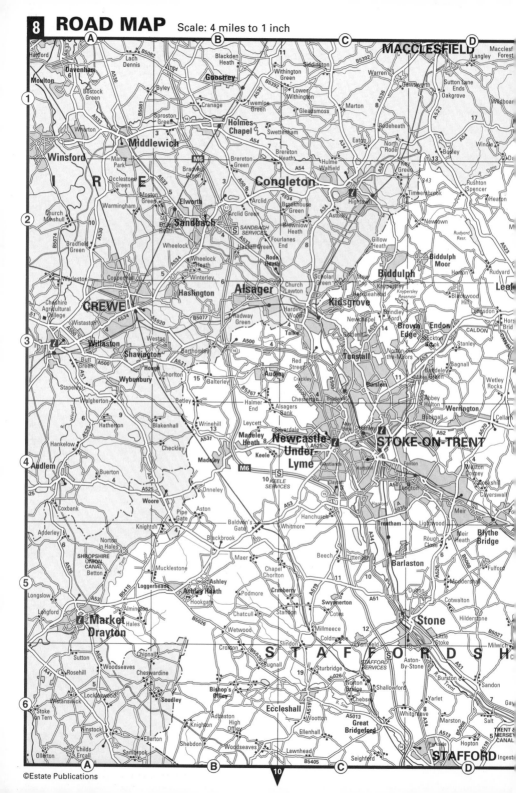

ROAD MAP Scale: 4 miles to 1 inch

8

MACCLESFIELD

©Estate Publications

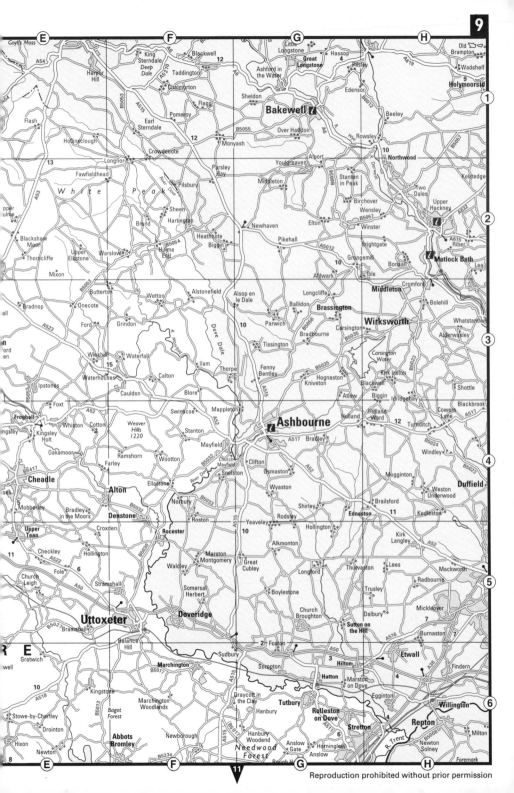

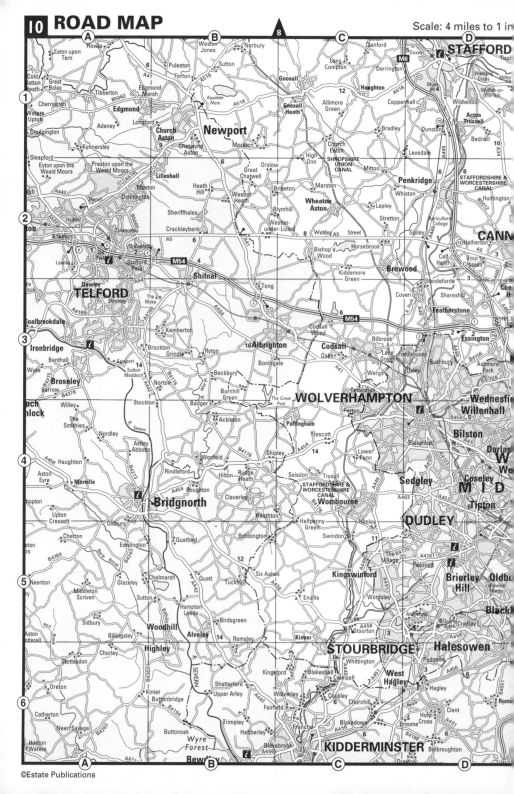

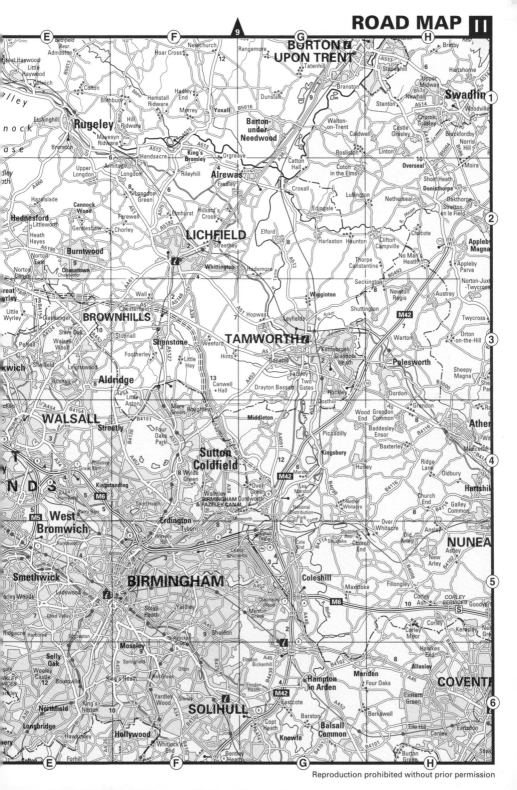

12 ALREWAS

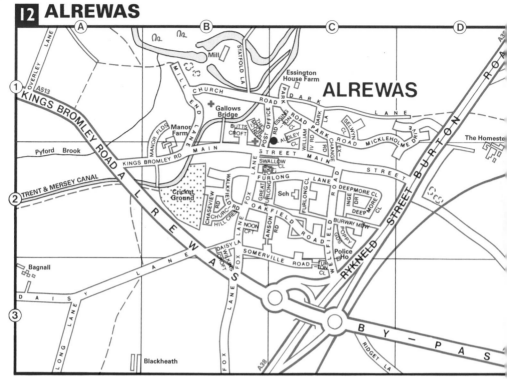

ALTON

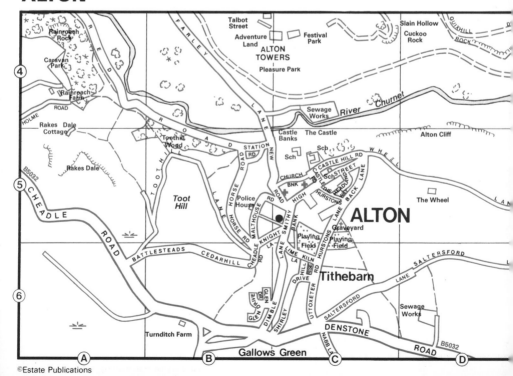

©Estate Publications

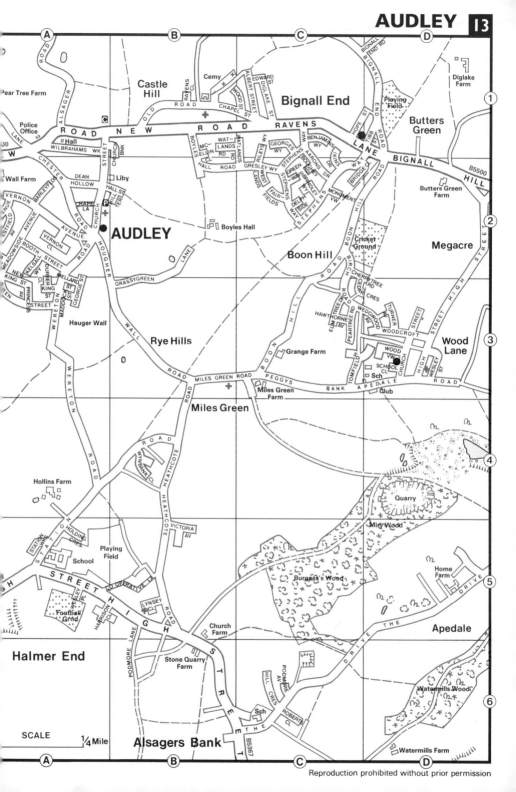

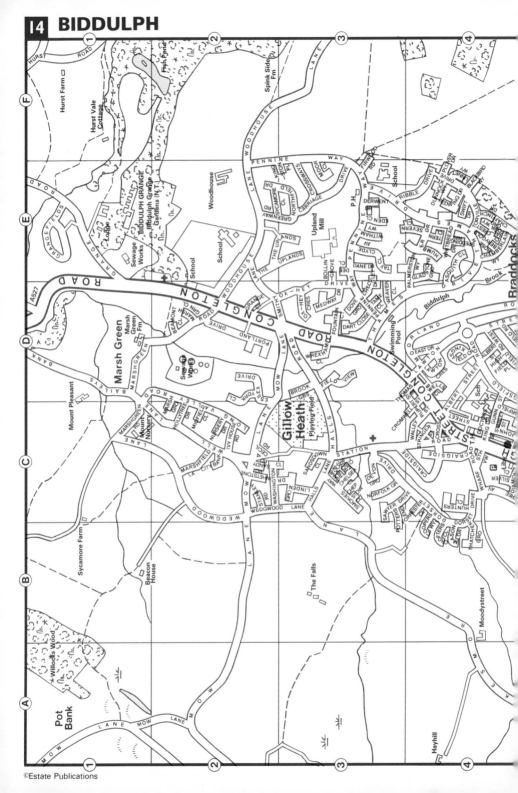

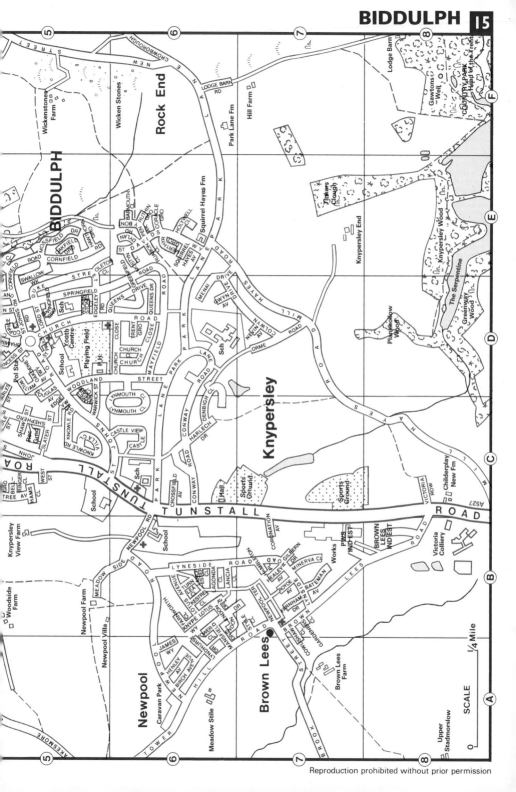

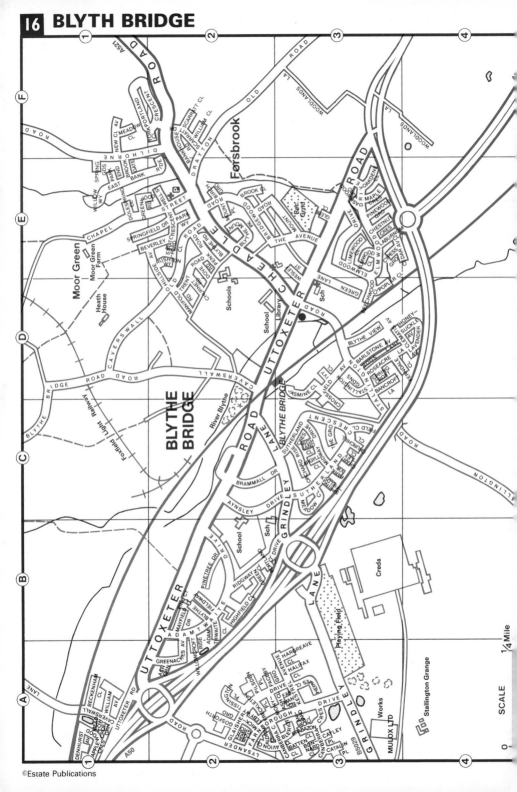

Forsbrook

Moor Green

BLYTHE BRIDGE

River Blythe

Creda

Playing Field

Stallington Grange

MULOX LTD

Works

SCALE

0   ¼ Mile

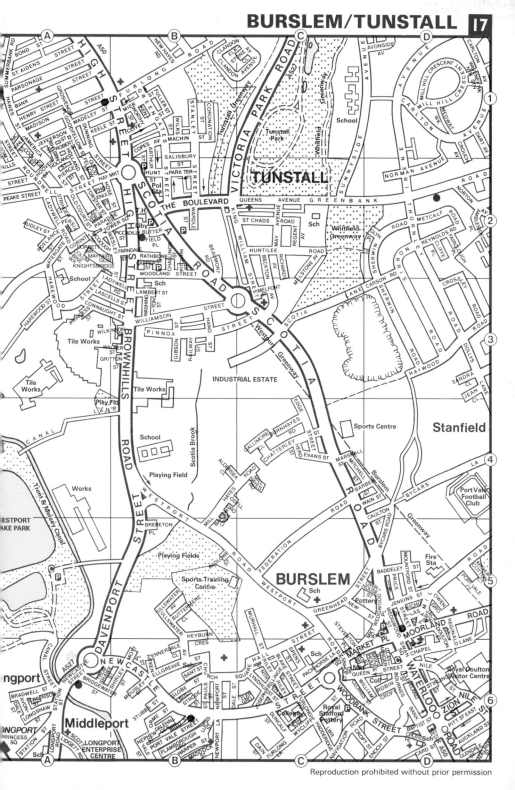

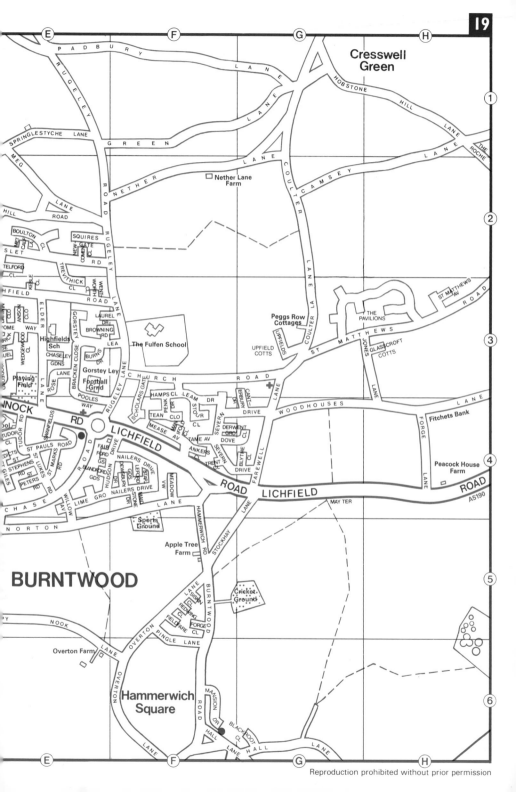

19

Cresswell Green

BURNTWOOD

Hammerwich Square

PADBURY LANE
RUGELEY ROAD
SPRINGLESTYCHE LANE
GREEN
HILL ROAD
MEG LANE
HILL
NETHER ROAD
Nether Lane Farm
HOBSTONE HILL LANE
THE ROCHE
CAMSEY LANE
COULTER LANE
BOULTON CL
SQUIRES
NEW GATE
COMET CL
RD
TREVITHICK CL
TELFORD CL
KEBLE
WORTH ROAD
ANSON CLO
ELDER LANE
WEDGEWOOD
GORSTEY LANE
LAUREL DRT
BROWNING RD
Highfields Sch
CHASELEY GDNS
BURNS DR
LEA
BRACKEN CLOSE
Gorstey Ley Football Grnd
ROSE LANE
POOLES WAY
SCHOLARS GATE
CHURCH
The Fulfen School
Peggs Row Cottages
UPFIELD COTTS
UPFIELDS
THE PAVILIONS
ST MATTHEWS AV
ROAD
ST MATTHEWS
JONES LANE
GLASSCROFT COTTS
FORGE LANE
Fitchets Bank
Peacock House Farm
Playing Field
HAMPS CL
LEAM DR
PENK
STOUR
TEAN CLO
MEASE AV
TAME AV
ANKERS CL
BLYTHE CL
SEVERN CL
SEVERN
DERWENT CLO
DOVE
CANT EBURY
DRIVE
WOODHOUSES ROAD
FAREWELL LANE
DRIVE
CANNOCK RD
LICHFIELD ROAD
SWANFIELDS
TUDOR CL
ST PAULS ROAD
ST MARKS RD
ST STEPHENS RD
ST LUKES RD
ST PETERS RD
ST GILES RD
BENEDICTS CL
FALB FORD GS
R BLANDFORD GDS
HUDSON DR
NAILERS DRIVE
LEPTON CL
PEMBURY
STONE
DEWSBURY GDS
MEADOW VW
MALL
CHASE
WILLOW AV
LIME GRO
NORTON
NAILERS DRIVE
MEADOW LANE
Sports Ground
HAMMERWICH RD
Apple Tree Farm
ROAD
LICHFIELD ROAD
STOCKHAY LANE
MAY TER
A5190
ROAD
NOOK
OVERTON LANE
Overton Farm
PINGLE LANE
BURNTWOOD ROAD
LASKEW
REDWING CL
FIELDFARE CL
FORGE CL
Cricket Ground
MANSION DR
BLACKROOT CL
HALL DR
HALL LANE
OVERTON ROAD

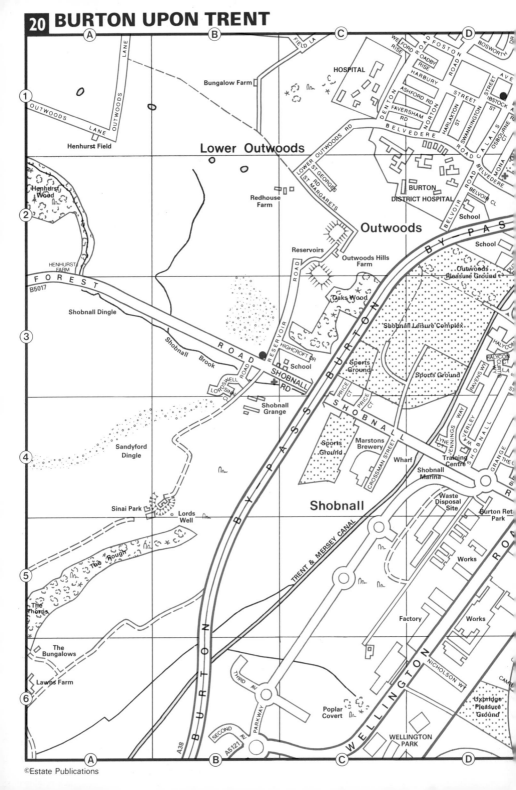

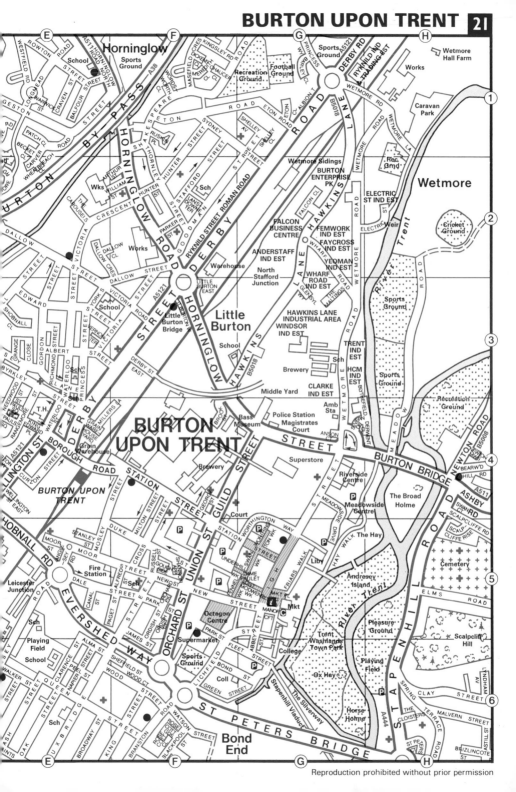

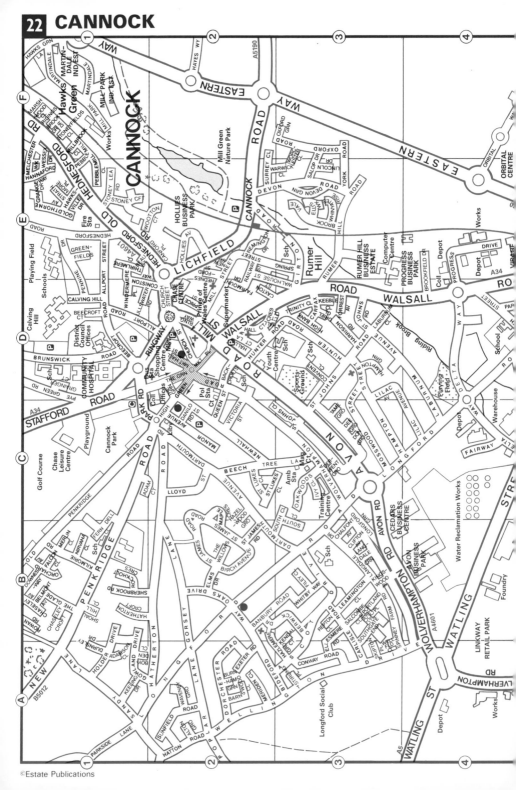

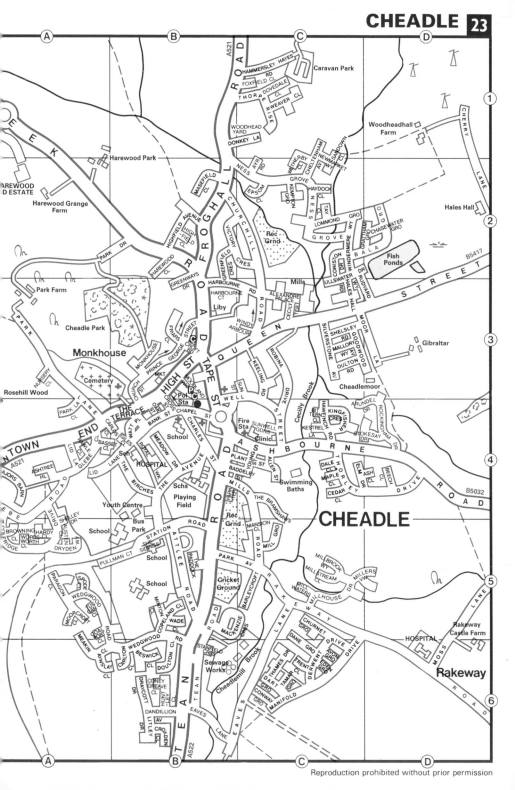

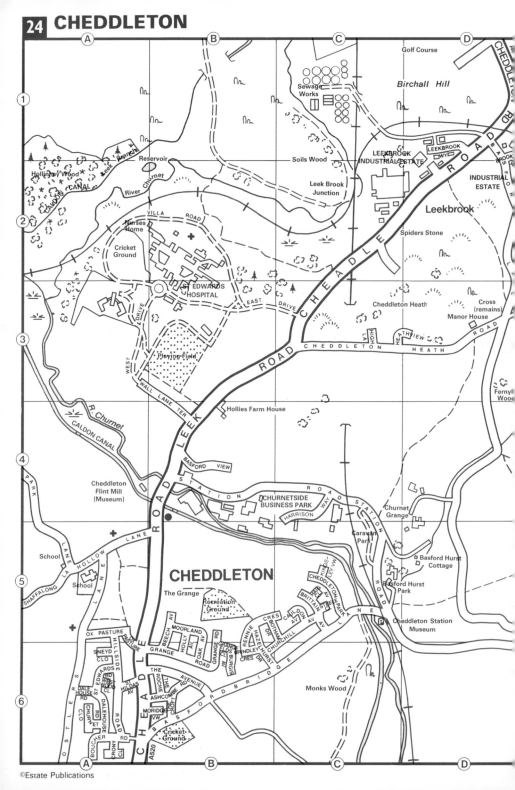

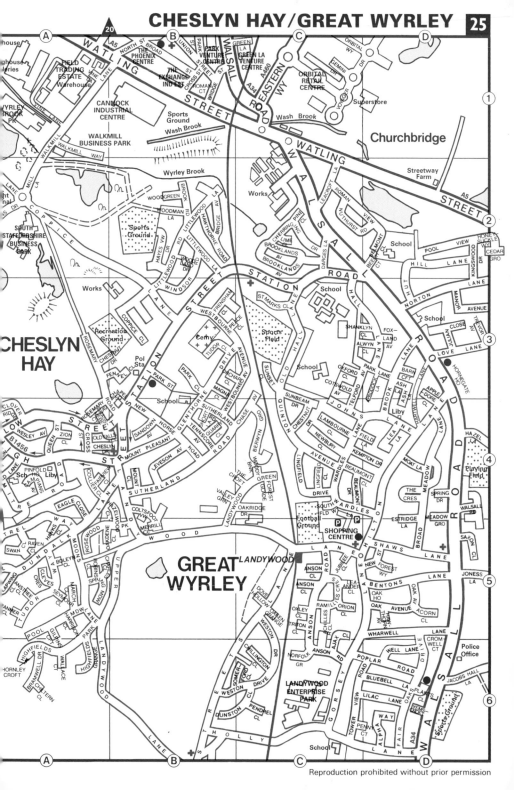

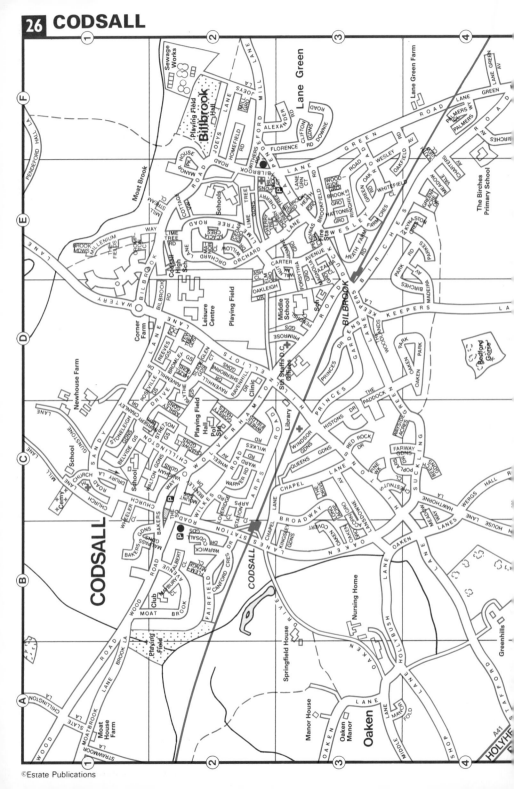

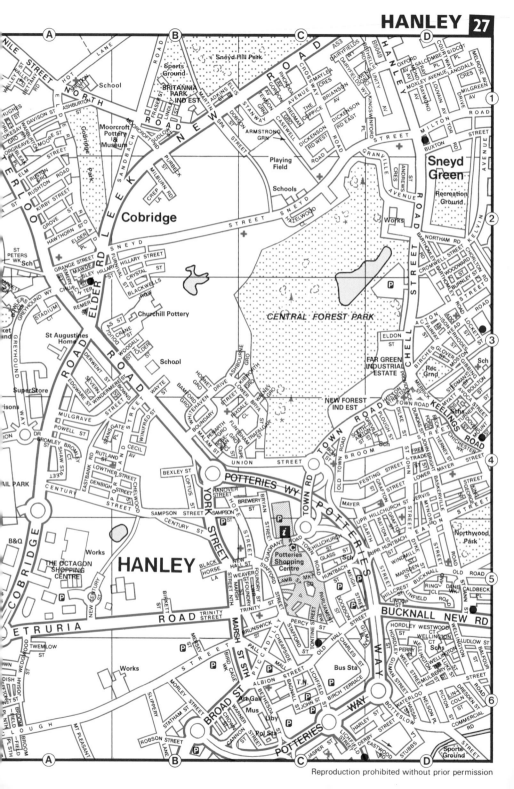

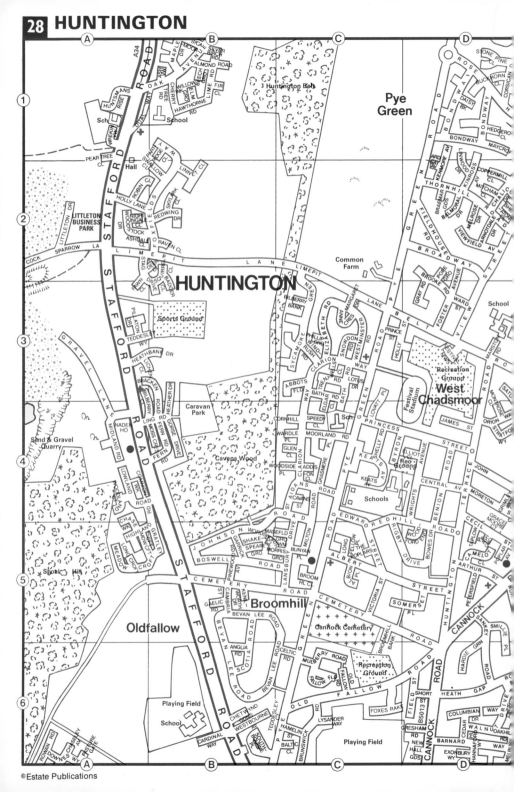

Pye Green

HUNTINGTON

West Chadsmoor

Broomhill

Oldfallow

Littleton Business Park

Common Farm

Sports Ground

Caravan Park

Cavens Wood

Sand & Gravel Quarry

Shoal Hill

Cannock Cemetery

Recreation Ground

Recreation Ground

Festival Stadium

Rec Ground

Schools

Huntington Belt

Playing Field

Playing Field

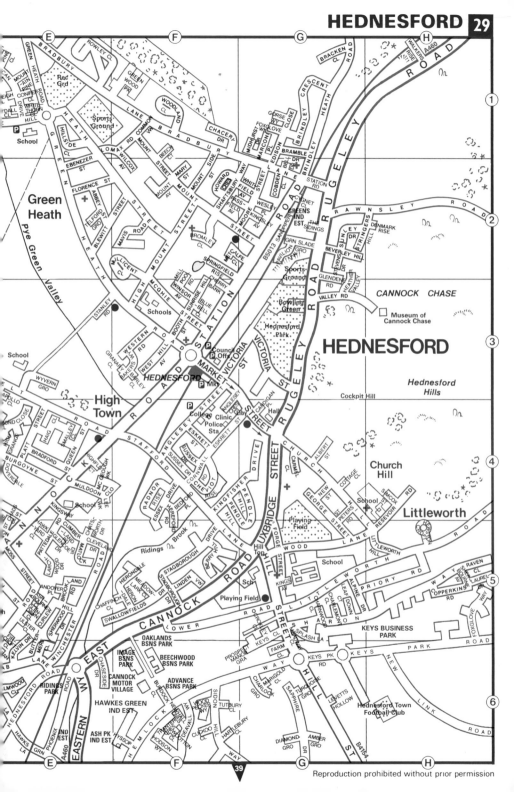

Green Heath

Pye Green Valley

HEDNESFORD

High Town

CANNOCK CHASE

Museum of Cannock Chase

Hednesford Hills

Cockpit Hill

Church Hill

Littleworth

KEYS BUSINESS PARK

Hednesford Town Football Club

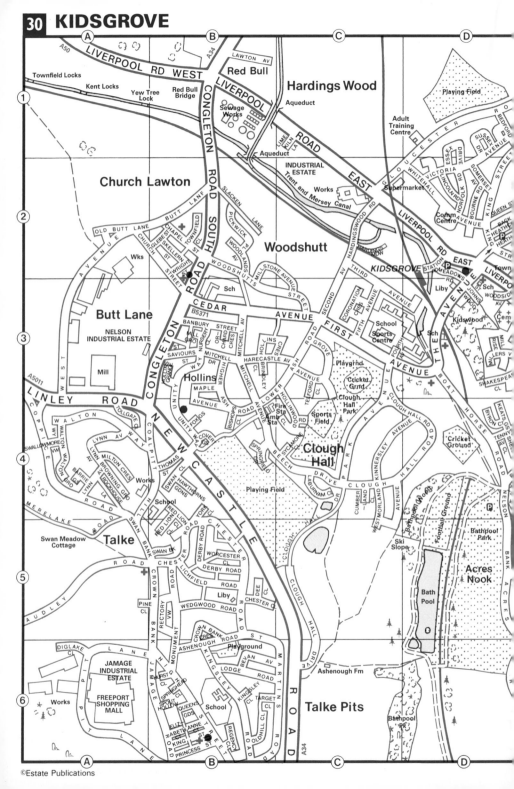

The Rookery

Newchapel

Natural Sciences Centre

Club

KIDSGROVE

LIVERPOOL ROAD

KIDSGROVE BANK

Birchen Wood

Gill Bank

Goldenhill Golf Course

Woodstock

Latebrook

Harecastle Tunnel

Goldenhill

School

Schools

Sports Ground

Sandyford

Ravenscliffe

Churchill Pottery

SCALE 0 1/4 Mile

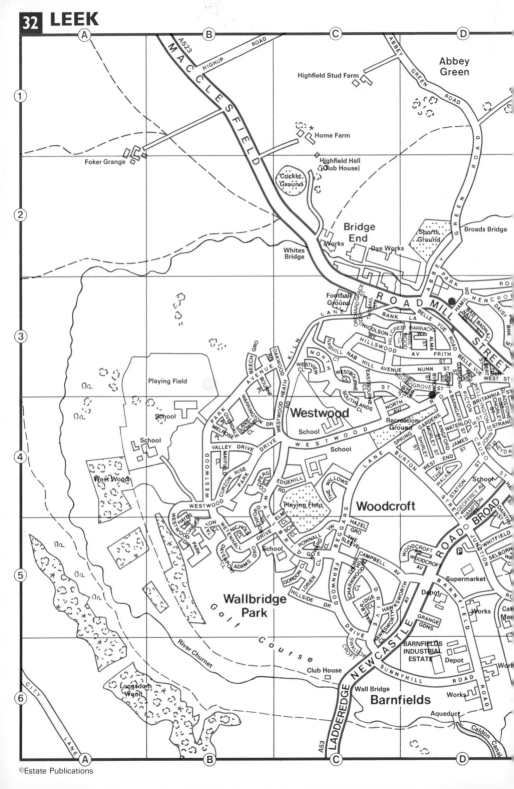

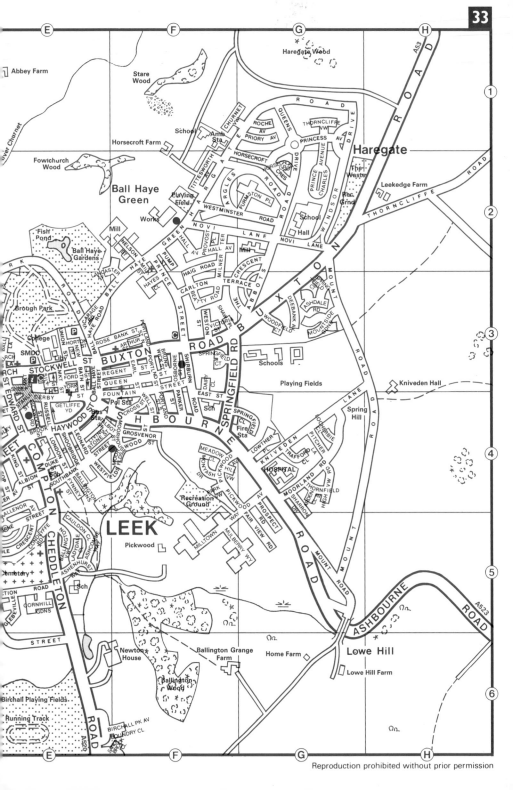

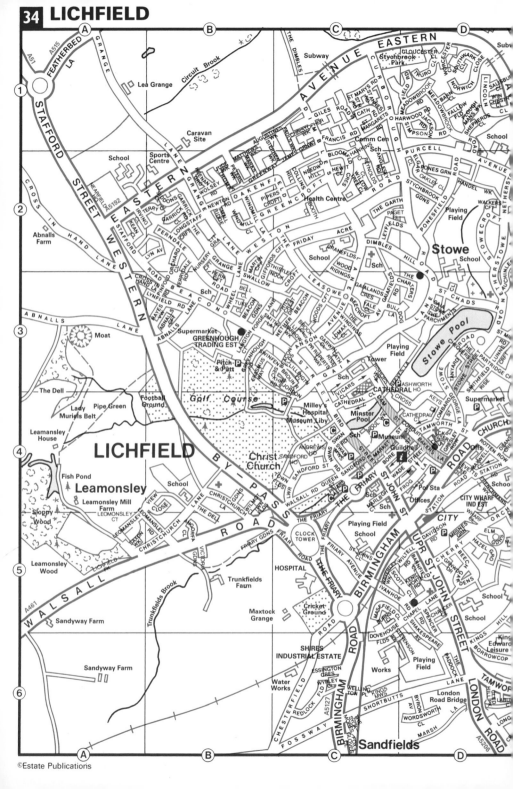

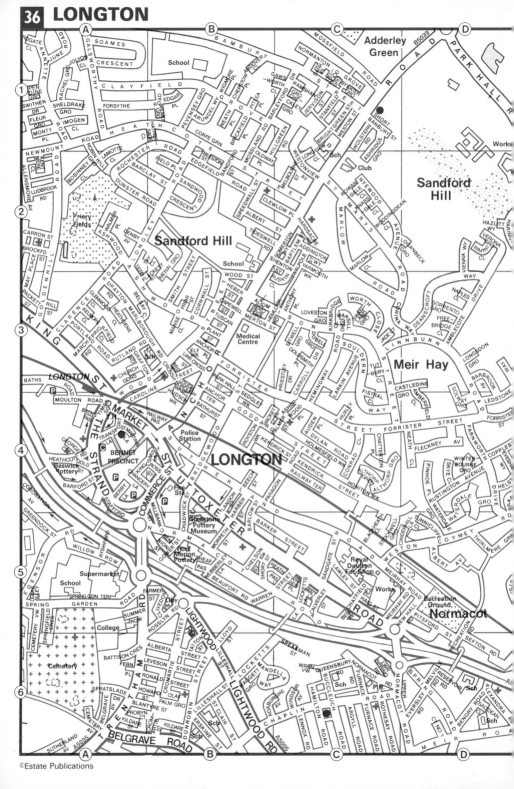

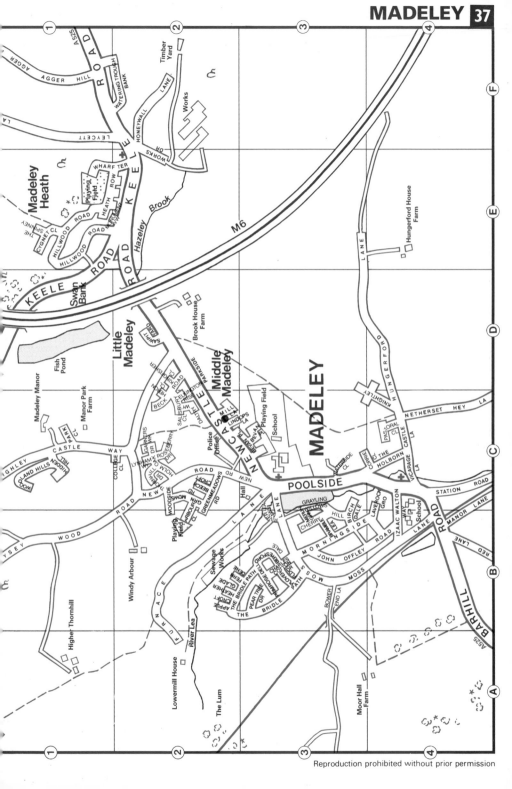

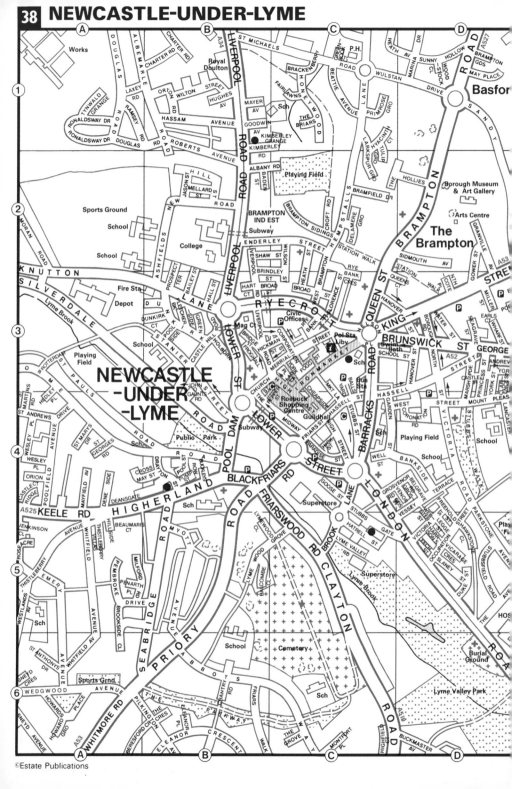

©Estate Publications

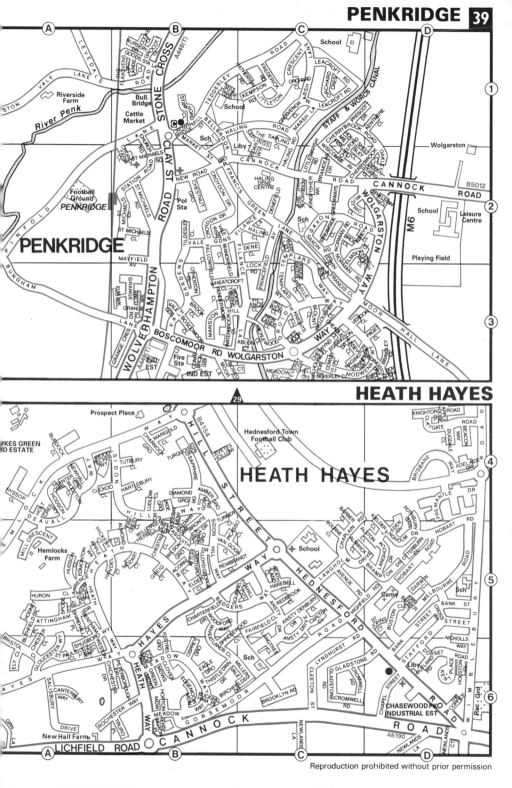

PENKRIDGE

HEATH HAYES

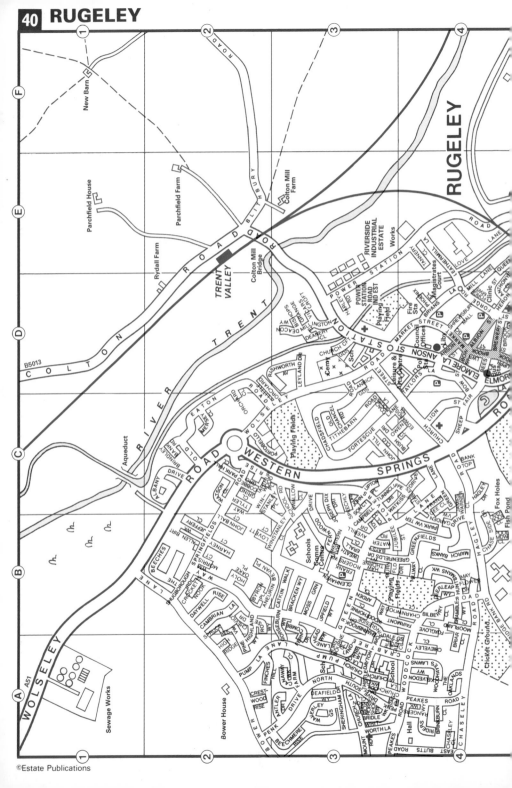

RUGELEY

©Estate Publications

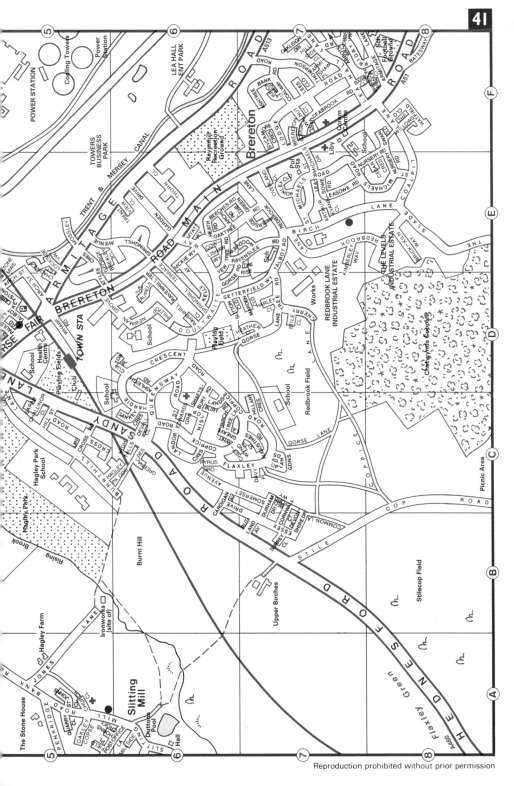

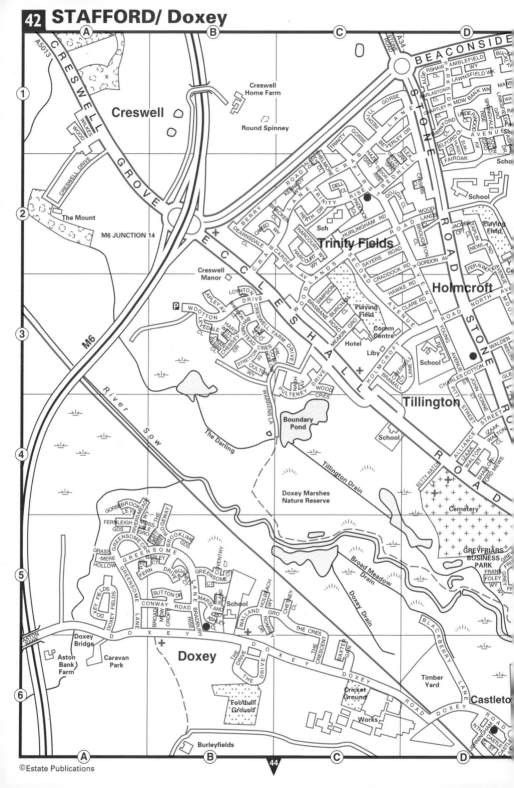

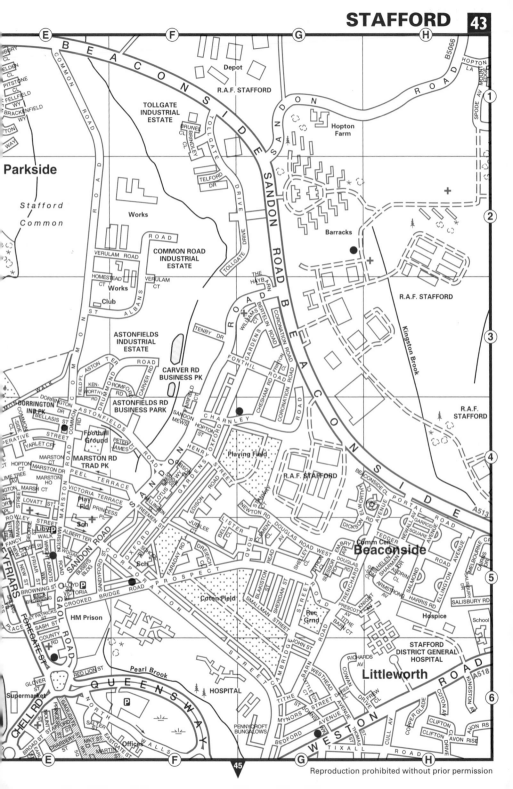

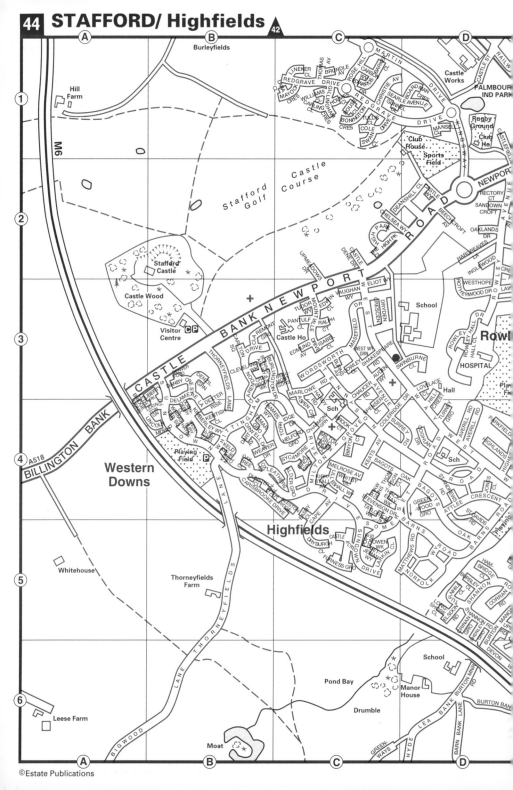

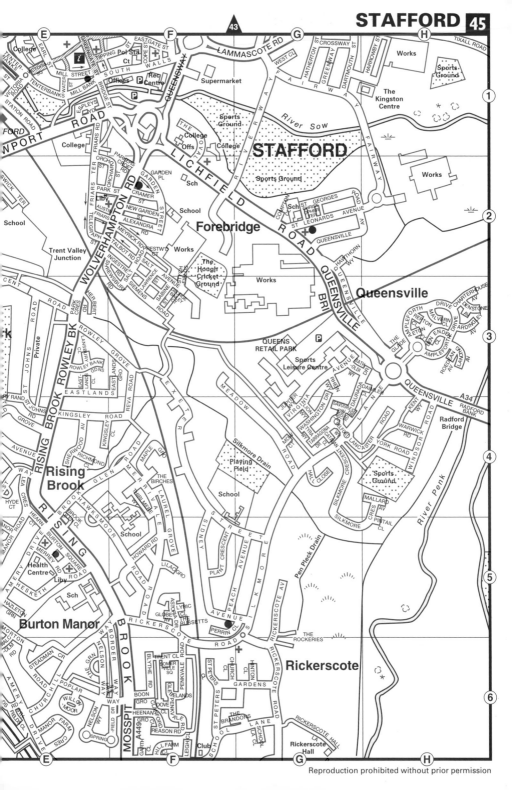

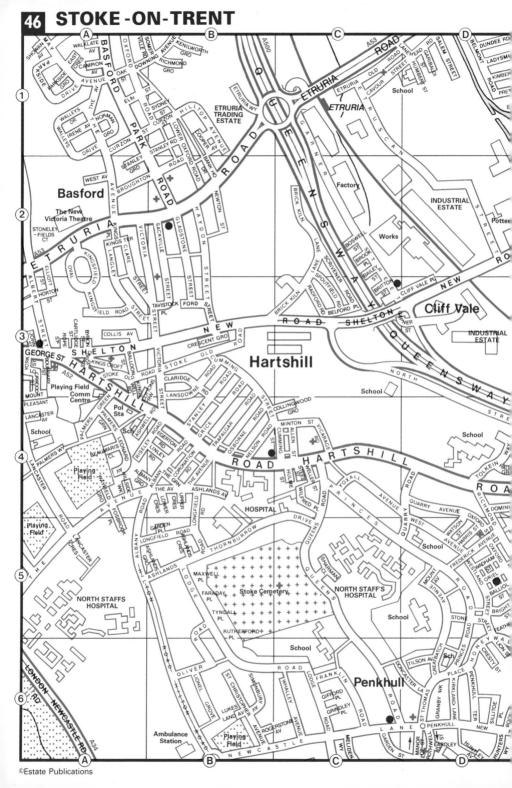

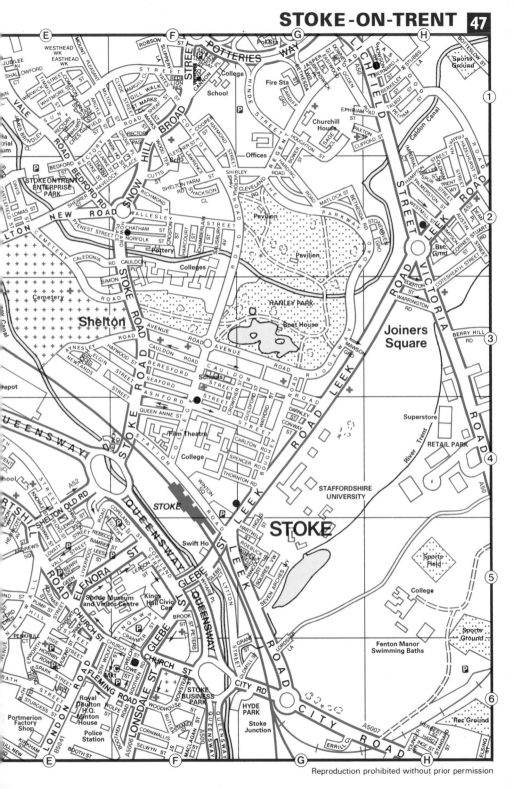

Oulton

Stonefield

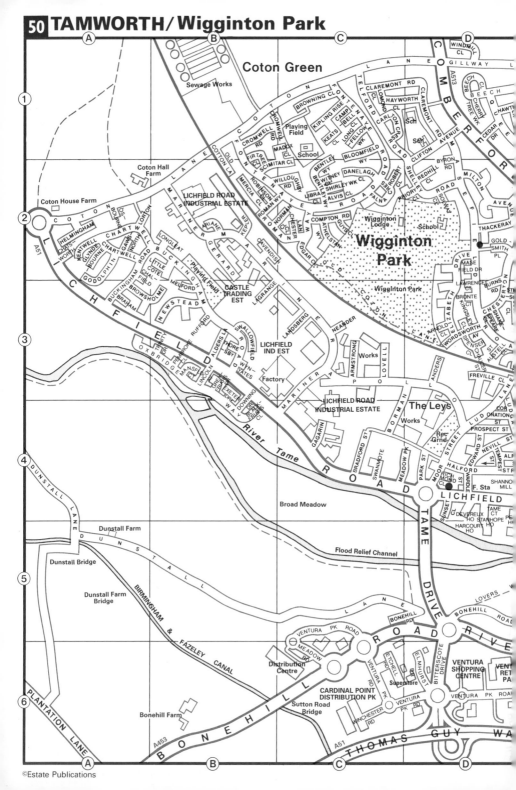

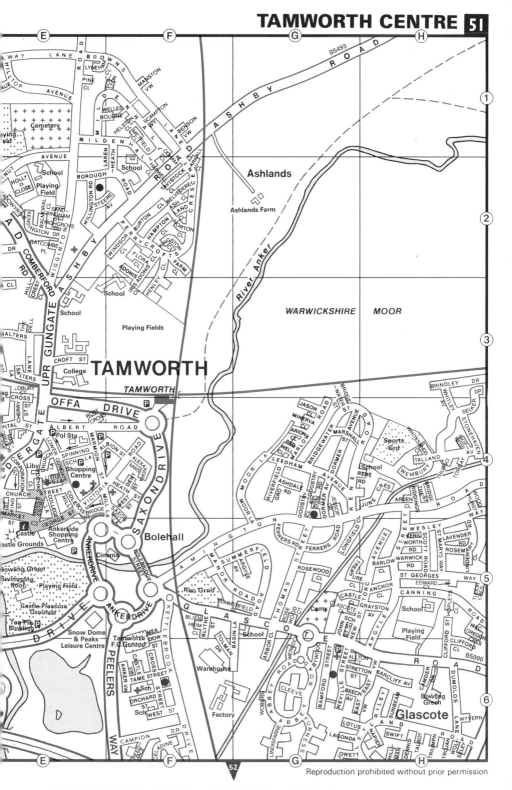

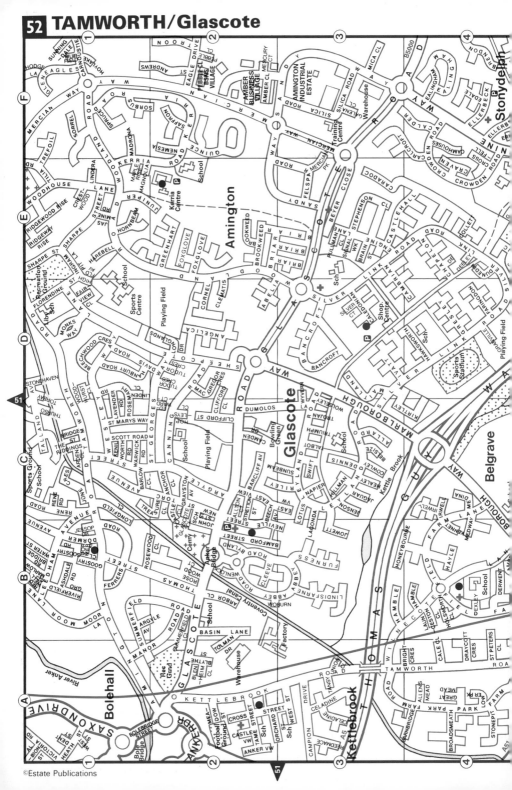

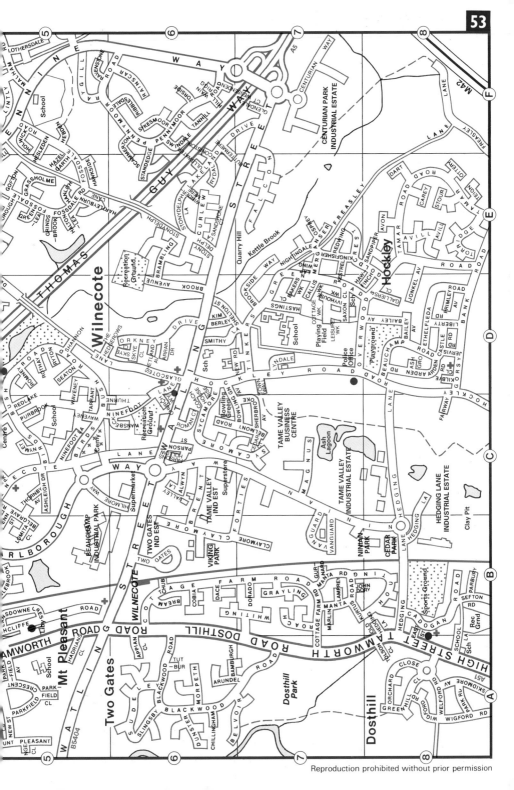

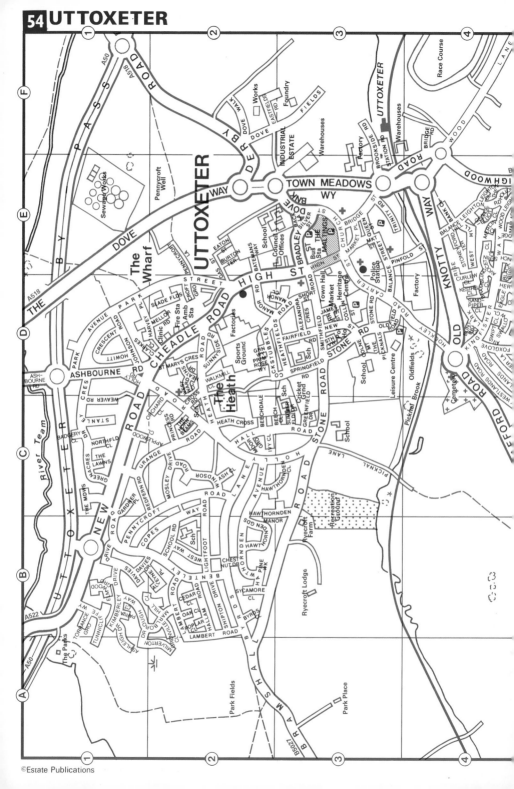

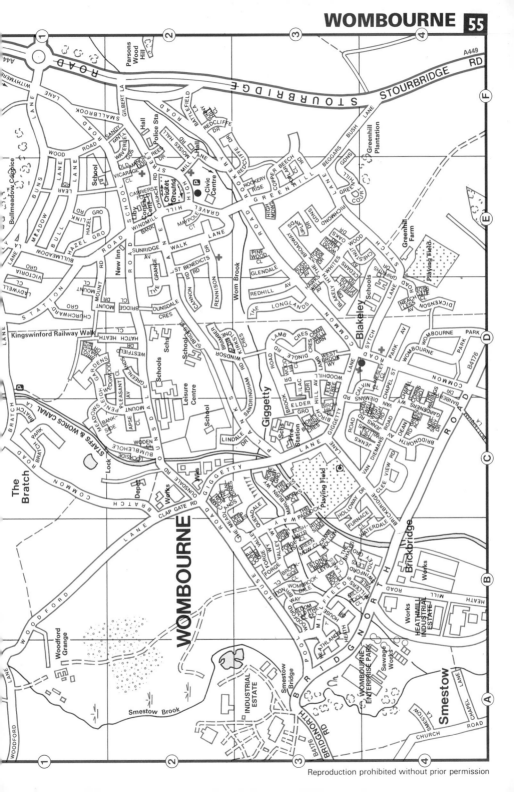

The Index includes some names for which there is insufficient space on the maps. These names are preceded by an * and are followed by the nearest adjoining thoroughfare.

Banchard Clo. ST3 16 A3
Beriot Clo. ST3 16 A3
the Bridge Rd. ST11 16 C1
the Clo. ST11 16 B2
the Mount Pk. ST11 16 E2
the Rd. ST11 16 E2
the View. ST11 16 D3
gs La. ST11 16 D3
nnard Clo. ST3 16 A3
abazon Clo. ST3 16 A3
ammall Dri. ST11 16 C2
idgwood Rd. ST11 16 E2
ook Clo. ST11 16 E2
ook Gate. ST11 16 E1
nberra Cres. ST3 16 A3
talina Pl. ST3 16 A3
verswall La. ST11 16 A1
verswall Old Rd.
ST11 16 D1
verswall Rd. ST11 16 D2
yley Pl. ST3 16 A3
dar Av. ST11 16 E3
apel St. ST11 16 E1
artley Clo. ST11 16 C3
eadle Pl. ST11 16 D3
estnut Cres. ST11 16 E3
urchill Clo. ST11 16 C3
urnet Rd. ST11 16 D2
ematis Av. ST11 16 D4
ossfield Av. ST11 16 D3
press Gro. ST11 16 E3
horne Rd. ST11 16 F2
elespring Clo. ST11 16 E1
ve Rd. ST11 16 E2
aycott Old Rd. ST11 16 E2
st Bank Ride. ST11 16 E1
lenhurst Av. ST3 16 A1
nwood Clo. ST11 16 E3
nwood Dri. ST11 16 E3
ceby Gro. ST3 16 A2
rman Clo. ST3 16 A3
rnborough Dri. ST3 16 A2
rndale Clo. ST11 16 A2
old Clo. ST11 16 C3
eldway. ST11 16 B2
eckleton Pl. ST3 16 A3
aisher Dri. ST3 16 A2
ebe Clo. ST3 16 E3
osforth Gro. ST3 16 A3
een Clo. ST11 16 B2
ea La. ST11 16 D3
eenacres Av. ST3 16 A2
eenwood Rd. ST11 16 E1
indley La. ST11 16 B3
alifax Clo. ST3 16 A3
argreave Clo. ST3 16 A3
ermes Clo. ST3 16 A3
ghfield Clo. ST11 16 B2
ghland Clo. ST11 16 C3
llside Av. ST11 16 D2
oneysuckle Av. ST11 16 D4
y Clo. ST11 16 D3
smine Clo. ST11 16 D3
estrel Av. ST3 16 A3
burnum Clo. ST11 16 E3
vender Av. ST11 16 D4
mewood Clo. ST11 16 E3
sander Rd. ST3 16 A2
anifold Rd. ST11 16 E3
aple Cres. ST11 16 E3
ayfield Dri. ST11 16 B2
eadow Clo,
Blythe Bridge. ST11 16 C3
eadow Clo,
Forsbrook. ST11 16 F1
eadowcroft Grn. ST3 16 A1
ickleby Way. ST3 16 C3
idway Dri. ST11 16 C3
onyash Clo. ST3 16 A3
ount Pl. ST11 16 E2
ount Rd. ST11 16 E3
ew Close Av. ST11 16 F1
akdene Clo. ST11 16 E3
rchard Rise. ST11 16 C3
ark End. ST11 16 E1
ark View. ST11 16 C3
ark Way. ST11 16 E2
enk Rd. ST11 16 E2
isden Pl. ST3 16 A2
ne La. ST11 16 B2
netree Dri. ST11 16 B2
nnewood Gro. ST11 16 E3
oplar Clo. ST11 16 D3
ortland Clo. ST11 16 F1
ortland Cres. ST11 16 F1
dgway Dri. ST11 16 D3
oseacre La. ST11 16 D3
ushton Way. ST11 16 E2
carratt Clo. ST11 16 F2
carratt Dri. ST11 16 F2
andy Croft. ST11 16 D3

Spring Gdns. ST11 16 E1
Springfield Dri. ST11 16 E2
Springfields. ST11 16 C1
Stallington Gdns. ST11 16 D3
Stallington Rd. ST11 16 C1
Stratford Clo. ST11 16 E2
Sutherland Cres. ST11 16 C3
The Avenue. ST11 16 E3
The Grove. ST11 16 E3
Tissington Pl. ST3 16 A2
Trent Rd. ST11 16 D2
Uttoxeter Rd. ST3 16 A1
Well St. ST11 16 E2
Wesley St. ST11 16 E3
William Av. ST3 16 A1
William Clo. ST11 16 F2
Willow Way. ST11 16 E1
Willowcroft Rise. ST11 16 A2
Woodlands La. ST11 16 F3
York Clo. ST11 16 F2

BURNTWOOD

Acorn Clo. WS7 18 C1
Albion Way. WS7 18 C2
Alden Hurst. WS7 18 B2
Amber Dri. WS7 18 C3
Angel Croft. WS7 18 A2
Anglesey Clo. WS7 18 B6
Ankers Clo. WS7 19 F4
Anson Clo. WS7 19 E3
Ash Grove. WS7 18 B5
Ashley Rd. WS7 18 A2
Ashmead Rd. WS7 18 D2
Aspen Gro. WS7 18 C2
Avon Rd. WS7 18 C5
Baker St. WS7 18 B4
Balmoral Way. WS7 18 A1
Bampton Av. WS7 18 A3
Bank Cres. WS7 18 C5
Barn Croft. WS7 18 C6
Baron Clo. WS7 18 B1
Beaudesert Rd. WS7 18 C1
Beech Cres. WS7 18 A1
Beechen Gro. WS7 18 B2
Bells La. WS7 18 C1
Belvedere Clo. WS7 18 B5
Benches Clo. WS7 18 A4
Biddulph Pk. WS7 18 A1
Birch Av. WS7 18 B5
Birch Ter. WS7 18 C1
Blackroot Clo. WS7 19 G6
Blackthorne Av. WS7 18 C6
Blandford Gdns. WS7 19 E4
Bleak House Dri. WS7 18 A2
Blenheim Rd. WS7 18 C2
Blythe Clo. WS7 19 G4
Boney Hay Rd. WS7 18 D2
Boulton Clo. WS7 19 E2
Bracken Clo. WS7 19 E3
Brackenhill. WS7 18 D2
Bramble La. WS7 18 D2
Brantwood Av. WS7 18 C5
Bridge Cross Rd. WS7 18 B3
Brook End. WS7 18 C6
Brooklyn Rd. WS7 18 C6
Browning Rd. WS7 19 E3
Brunel Clo. WS7 18 D2
Burleigh Cres. WS7 18 B2
Burns Dri. WS7 19 E3
Burntwood Rd. WS7 19 F5
Byron Clo. WS7 18 C1
Californian Gro. WS7 18 B2
Camsey La. WS7 19 G2
Cannel Rd. WS7 18 A4
Cannock Rd. WS7 18 A3
Cannock Rd,
Burntwood. WS7 18 D3
Canterbury Dri. WS7 19 G3
Carlton Cres. WS7 18 C2
Cedar Clo. WS7 18 C4
Cedar Rd. WS7 18 C4
Chapel St. WS7 18 A2
Chase Rd. WS7 18 C5
Chase Vale. WS7 18 B4
Chaselands. WS7 18 A3
Chaseley Gdns. WS7 19 E3
Chaucer Clo. WS7 18 C1
Chawner Clo. WS7 18 A1
Cherry Clo. WS7 18 C4
Chorley Rd. WS7 18 B1
Church Rd. WS7 19 F3
Church St. WS7 18 A5
Clinton Cres. WS7 18 D2
Clive Rd. WS7 18 D3
Columbian Cres. WS7 18 B2
Common Vw. WS7 18 C1
Coppice Clo. WS7 18 B2

Coppy Nook La. WS7 18 D5
Copthorne Av. WS7 18 C6
Corsican Clo. WS7 18 C2
Cort Dri. WS7 18 D2
Cottage Clo. WS7 18 B5
Cottage La. WS7 18 B5
Cotton Way. WS7 18 B2
Coulson Clo. WS7 18 A1
Coulter La. WS7 19 G2
Crane Dri. WS7 18 C6
Cranfield Rd. WS7 18 D3
Croft Gdns. WS7 18 D2
Cross St. WS7 18 B2
Cumberland Cres. WS7 18 C2
Dale Dri. WS7 18 D3
Darwin Clo. WS7 19 E3
Deal Av. WS7 18 C2
Deerfold Cres. WS7 18 D3
Derwent Gro. WS7 19 F4
Dewsbury Dri. WS7 19 F4
Dove Clo. WS7 19 F4
Duke Rd. WS7 18 B1
Dunston Dri. WS7 18 C2
Dursley Rd. WS7 18 C3
Earls Dri. WS7 18 B1
Eastcote Cres. WS7 18 C5
Eastgate St. WS7 18 A2
Eastwood Av. WS7 18 D2
Edwards Rd. WS7 18 B5
Elder La. WS7 19 E3
Elmhurst Dri. WS7 18 C6
Elunda Gro. WS7 18 A5
Emmanuel Rd. WS7 18 D3
Fair Lady Dri. WS7 18 A2
Fairford Gdns. WS7 19 E4
Farewell La. WS7 19 G4
Ferndale Clo. WS7 18 D4
Fernleigh Av. WS7 18 C2
Fieldfare. WS7 19 F5
Fieldhouse Rd. WS7 18 C3
Filton Av. WS7 18 D2
Forge Clo. WS7 19 F5
Forge La. WS7 19 H4
Foxcroft Clo. WS7 18 D5
Foxhills. WS7 18 C5
Franklin Dri. WS7 18 D4
Galway Rd. WS7 18 C3
Garrick Rise. WS7 19 E3
Glasscroft Cotts. WS7 19 H3
Glenmore Av. WS7 18 D4
Gorseway. WS7 18 D5
Gorstey Lea. WS7 19 E3
Grange Av. WS7 18 D4
Grange Rd. WS7 18 C5
Green La. WS7 19 F1
Griffin Clo. WS7 18 A3
Hall La. WS7 19 F6
Halston Rd. WS7 18 D3
Hammerwich Rd. WS7 19 F4
Hamps Clo. WS7 19 F3
Hanney Hay Rd. WS7 18 D6
Hawthorne Cres. WS7 18 C4
Hazelmere Dri. WS7 18 B6
Heath Vw. WS7 18 C1
Henley Clo. WS7 18 D5
High St,
Chase Terrace. WS7 18 A2
High St,
Chasetown. WS7 18 B4
Highfield Av. WS7 18 D3
Highfield Clo. WS7 18 D3
Highfield Rd. WS7 18 D3
Highfields. WS7 18 D3
Highfields Rd. WS7 18 B6
Hill La. WS7 18 B1
Hill St. WS7 18 B5
Hillcrest Rise. WS7 18 D6
Hobstone Hill La. WS7 19 G1
Holly Grove La. WS7 18 A1
Hospital Rd. WS7 18 D6
Hudson Dri. WS7 19 E4
Hunslet Rd. WS7 18 D2
Hunter Av. WS7 19 E3
Huntsmans Gate. WS7 18 D2

INDUSTRIAL & RETAIL:

Acorn Starter Units.
WS7 18 A3
Burntwood Shopping
Centre. WS7 18 A3
Chase Pk Ind Est.
WS7 18 A3
Chasetown Ind Est.
WS7 18 A4
Mount Rd Ind Est.
WS7 18 D4
Ironstone Rd. WS7 18 A1
James Hutchens Ct.
WS7 18 B5
Jerome Way. WS7 19 E3
Johnson Rd. WS7 18 C2
Jones La. WS7 19 H3

Keble Clo. WS7 19 E3
Keepers Clo. WS7 18 D4
King St. WS7 18 B5
Kingsdown Rd. WS7 18 A1
Kipling Av. WS7 18 C2
Knight Rd. WS7 18 B1
Knoll Clo. WS7 18 C5
Laburnum Gro. WS7 18 C4
Larkspur Av. WS7 18 D5
Laurel Dri. WS7 19 E3
Lawnswood Av. WS7 18 B5
Lea Hall Dri. WS7 18 A1
Leafdene Av. WS7 18 C4
Leam Dri. WS7 19 F3
Leander Clo. WS7 18 A1
Lebanon Gro. WS7 18 B2
Leigh Av. WS7 18 D3
Lichfield Rd. WS7 19 F4
Lilac Gro. WS7 18 C3
Lime Gro. WS7 18 C4
Linden Av. WS7 18 C2
Littleton Way. WS7 18 A1
Loftus Ct. WS7 18 C5
Lodge Rd. WS7 18 B1
Lombardy Gro. WS7 18 B2
Longfellow Rd. WS7 18 C1
Lorne St. WS7 18 A2
Lulworth Rd. WS7 18 C3
Lymington Rd. WS7 18 B1
Macadam Clo. WS7 18 D2
Maidstone Dri. WS7 19 F4
Manifold Clo. WS7 19 F4
Manor Rise. WS7 18 C5
Mansion Dri. WS7 19 F6
Maple Clo. WS7 18 B3
Marton Av. WS7 18 D2
Masefield Clo. WS7 18 C2
Mavor Av. WS7 18 A1
May Clo. WS7 18 C1
May Ter. WS7 19 G4
Meadow Vw. WS7 19 F4
Meadway St. WS7 18 C5
Mease Av. WS7 19 F4
Meg La. WS7 18 D1
Melford Rise. WS7 18 B1
Melrose. WS7 18 C5
Metcalf La. WS7 19 E2
Millett Av. WS7 18 B6
Morley Rd. WS7 18 D3
Morlings Dri. WS7 18 D2
Moss Bank Av. WS7 18 D4
Mount Rd. WS7 18 D5
Mowbray Croft. WS7 18 A1
Myatt Av. WS7 18 C3
Nailers Dri. WS7 19 F4
Nether La. WS7 19 F2
New Rd. WS7 18 D5
New St,
Chase Terrace. WS7 18 B2
New St,
Chasetown. WS7 18 B5
Newcomen Clo. WS7 18 C5
Newgate St. WS7 18 C5
No Name Rd. WS7 18 A3
North St. WS7 18 B1
Norton La. WS7 19 E5
Oak La. WS7 18 C1
Oakdene Rd. WS7 18 C4
Oaken Gdns. WS7 18 C4
Oatfield Clo. WS7 18 C6
Ogley Hay Rd. WS7 18 B1
Ogley Hay Rd. WS7 18 D6
Oregon Gdns. WS7 18 C2
Overhill Rd. WS7 18 D5
Overton La. WS7 19 F6
Padbury La. WS7 19 E1
Paget Dri. WS7 18 A1
Park Av. WS7 18 D5
Park Rd,
Burntwood. WS7 18 D5
Park Rd,
Chase Terrace. WS7 18 B2
Parkhill Rd. WS7 18 C2
Paviers Rd. WS7 18 B6
Penk Dri. WS7 19 F4
Pine Gro. WS7 18 C4
Pingle La. WS7 19 F5
Plant La. WS7 18 A3
Pool Rd. WS7 18 A6
Pooles Way. WS7 19 E3
Poplar Av. WS7 18 C4
Princess Clo. WS7 18 A3
Princess St. WS7 18 A3
Prospect Rd. WS7 18 D4
Queens Dri. WS7 18 C4
Queens St. WS7 18 B5
Radmore Clo. WS7 18 A2
Railway La. WS7 18 B1
Rake Hill. WS7 19 F4
Rake Hill Rd. WS7 19 F4
Redfern Dri. WS7 18 D5

Redwing Clo. WS7 19 F5
Redwood Dri. WS7 18 B2
Ring Rd. WS7 18 A3
Robins Rd. WS7 18 A4
Robinson Rd. WS7 18 B2
Rochester Av. WS7 18 C3
Rose La. WS7 19 E3
Rowan Gro. WS7 18 C3
Rugeley La. WS7 19 F2
Rugeley Rd,
Burntwood. WS7 19 E1
Rugeley Rd,
Chase Terrace. WS7 18 B2
Russett Clo. WS7 18 D5
Ryecroft Dri. WS7 18 C2
St Annes Clo. WS7 18 B6
St Benedicts. WS7 19 E4
St Giles Rd. WS7 19 F4
St Lukes Rd. WS7 19 E4
St Marks Rd. WS7 19 F4
St Matthews Av. WS7 19 H2
St Matthews Rd. WS7 19 G3
St Pauls Rd. WS7 19 F4
St Peters Rd. WS7 19 F4
St Stephens Rd. WS7 19 E4
Sanderling Rise. WS7 18 D2
Sandown Clo. WS7 18 B1
Sandringham Clo. WS7 18 A1
Scholars Gate. WS7 19 F4
School Clo. WS7 18 A2
School La. WS7 18 A2
School Walk. WS7 18 A2
Scott Way. WS7 18 C2
Segemoor Av. WS7 18 B5
Severn Dri. WS7 19 F4
Shakespeare Rd. WS7 18 B2
Shaw Dri. WS7 18 C1
Shirelea Clo. WS7 18 D3
Siskin Clo. WS7 19 F5
Slade Av. WS7 18 C2
Smiths Clo. WS7 18 A4
Spencer Dri. WS7 18 B2
Spinney Clo. WS7 18 C1
Spinney La. WS7 18 B1
Spring Hill Rd. WS7 18 C4
Springlestyche La. WS7 19 E1
Squires Gate. WS7 19 E2
Squirrells Hollow. WS7 18 C1
Stamford Cres. WS7 18 C2
Stapleford Gdns. WS7 19 F4
Stockhay La. WS7 19 F5
Stour Clo. WS7 19 F4
Summerfield Rd. WS7 18 C5
Sunnymead Rd. WS7 18 E3
Swanfields. WS7 19 E4
Sycamore Rd. WS7 18 B3
Tame Av. WS7 19 F4
Tean Clo. WS7 19 F4
Telford Clo. WS7 19 E2
Tennyson Av. WS7 18 C1
The Crescent. WS7 18 B1
The Orchard. WS7 18 B4
The Pavilions. WS7 19 G3
The Ridgeway. WS7 18 C5
The Roche. WS7 19 H1
Thistledown Av. WS7 18 C2
Thornfield Cres. WS7 18 C2
Thorpe Av. WS7 18 A2
Thorpe Clo. WS7 18 A2
Thorpe St. WS7 18 A3
Travellers Clo. WS7 18 D5
Trent Clo. WS7 19 F4
Trevern Dri. WS7 18 B5
Trevithick Clo. WS7 19 E2
Tudor Clo. WS7 19 E4
Tudor Rd. WS7 19 E4
Union St. WS7 18 B5
Upfield Cotts. WS7 19 G3
Upfields. WS7 19 G3
Victory Av. WS7 18 B3
Viscount Rd. WS7 18 B1
Warren Rd. WS7 18 D5
Water St. WS7 18 B2
Wedgewood Clo. WS7 19 E3
Wentworth Clo. WS7 19 E3
Wesley Clo. WS7 18 B1
*Westbourne Cres,
Hunter Av. WS7 19 E3
Westwoods Hollow.
WS7 18 D2
Wharf La. WS7 18 C6
Wheatcroft Clo. WS7 18 D5
Whitehouse Cres. WS7 18 D3
Wilkinson Clo. WS7 18 D2
Willow Av. WS7 19 E4
Windsor Clo. WS7 18 A1
Woodford Cres. WS7 18 C5
Woodhouse La. WS7 19 G4
Woodland Way. WS7 18 C1
Wordsworth Rd. WS7 18 C1

BURSLEM/ TUNSTALL

Adelaide St. ST6 17 D6
Aitken St. ST6 17 B6
Alderse Clo. ST6 17 B4
Ambleside Pl. ST6 17 D2
America St. ST6 17 A1
Arthur Cotton Ct. ST6 17 D5
Arthur St. ST6 17 B1
Athelstan St. ST6 17 A1
Auckland St. ST6 17 D6
Audley St. ST6 17 A2
Avondale St. ST6 17 A6
Avonside Av. ST6 17 D1
Baddeley St. ST6 17 D5
Bank St. ST6 17 A1
Baptist St. ST6 17 D6
Barber St. ST6 17 C4
Barton Cres. ST6 17 B4
Beaumont Rd. ST6 17 B2
Beckton Av. ST6 17 C2
Billinge St. ST6 17 C6
Blake St. ST6 17 C6
Bond St. ST6 17 A1
Bournes Bank. ST6 17 D6
*Bournes Bank Sth, Baptist St. ST6 17 D6
Bradwell St. ST6 17 A6
Brereton Pl. ST6 17 B5
Brickhouse St. ST6 17 D6
Bridgewater St. ST6 17 A6
Broomhill St. ST6 17 A1
Brownhills Rd. ST6 17 B3
Bulstrode St. ST6 17 B6
Burnhayes Rd. ST6 17 C4
Butterfield Pl. ST6 17 B2
Buttermere Clo. ST6 17 B5
Bycars La. ST6 17 D4
Bycars Rd. ST6 17 D5
Calver St. ST6 17 A2
Canal La. ST6 17 A4
Canal St. ST6 17 A6
Capper St. ST6 17 B2
Card St. ST6 17 D6
Carlton Av. ST6 17 D1
Carson Rd. ST6 17 D3
Caulton St. ST6 17 D4
Challinor St. ST6 17 B2
Chapel La. ST6 17 D6
Chatterley St. ST6 17 C4
Church Sq. ST6 17 B6
Clandon Av. ST6 17 B1
Clay Hills. ST6 17 A2
Clayhanger St. ST6 17 D6
Cleveland St. ST6 17 D6
Cliffe Pl. ST6 17 D2
Clive St. ST6 17 B1
Columbine Walk. ST6 17 A2
Connaught St. ST6 17 A3
Coolidge St. ST6 17 A1
Copes Av. ST6 17 B1
Corbett Walk. ST6 17 A2
Corinth Way. ST6 17 A2
Coronation St. ST6 17 B1
Croft St. ST6 17 C6
Cross Hill. ST6 17 D6
Crossley Rd. ST6 17 D3
Crouch Av. ST6 17 D1
Dain St. ST6 17 C6
Dale St. ST6 17 B6
Dalehall Gdns. ST6 17 B6
Dart Av. ST6 17 D1
Davenport St. ST6 17 A6
Dollys La. ST6 17 D3
Doulton St. ST6 17 D5
Duncalf St. ST6 17 C6
Dunning St. ST6 17 A1
Edge St. ST6 17 C4
Ellgreave St. ST6 17 B6
Ennerdale Clo. ST6 17 B6
Enoch St. ST6 17 D6
Evans St. ST6 17 C4
Fairclough Pl. ST6 17 D2
Farndale St. ST6 17 B2
Federation Rd. ST6 17 C5
Flamborough Gro. ST6 17 B6
Forster St. ST6 17 A2
Fountain Sq. ST6 17 C6
Fuller St. ST6 17 B1
Furlong La. ST6 17 C6
Furlong Par. ST6 17 C6
Furlong Rd. ST6 17 B1
Furlong View. ST6 17 C6
Gallimore Clo. ST6 17 C4
Gibson St. ST6 17 B3
Glendale St. ST6 17 D6
Globe St. ST6 17 B6
Glyn Pl. ST6 17 D2
Goodfellow St. ST6 17 A1
Greenbank Rd. ST6 17 C2
Greengates St. ST6 17 B1
Greenhead St. ST6 17 C5
Gritton St. ST6 17 B3
Grosvenor Pl. ST6 17 A1
Hall St. ST6 17 C6
Hamil Rd. ST6 17 D5
Hand St. ST6 17 B3
Harewood St. ST6 17 A3
Harper St. ST6 17 B6
Hawes St. ST6 17 A1
Hay Mkt. ST6 17 A2
Haywood Rd. ST6 17 D3
Henry St. ST6 17 A1
Herd St. ST6 17 C4
Heyburn Cres. ST6 17 B5
High St. ST6 17 A1
Holland St. ST6 17 A2
Hoover St. ST6 17 A2
Hose St. ST6 17 A2
Hunt St. ST6 17 B2
Huntilee Rd. ST6 17 C2

INDUSTRIAL & RETAIL:

Longport Enterprise Centre. ST6 17 A6
Irene Av. ST6 17 D2
Jackson St. ST6 17 D5
Jacqueline St. ST6 17 A1
Jean Clo. ST6 17 D3
Jefferson St. ST6 17 A1
Jenkins St. ST6 17 D5
Joseph St. ST6 17 C6
Keele St. ST6 17 A1
Kenworthy St. ST6 17 B1
King William St. ST6 17 B2
Knight St. ST6 17 A1
Knightsbridge Way. ST6 17 A2
Ladywell Rd. ST6 17 A2
Lambert St. ST6 17 B3
Lascells St. ST6 17 A3
Longport Rd. ST6 17 A6
Longshaw St. ST6 17 A6
Lower Hadderidge. ST6 17 C6
Lucas St. ST6 17 B6
Lyndhurst St. ST6 17 C6
McGough St. ST6 17 A2
Machin St. ST6 17 B1
McKinley St. ST6 17 A1
Maddock St. ST6 17 B6
Madeley St. ST6 17 A1
Madison St. ST6 17 A1
Market Pass. ST6 17 C6
Market Pl. ST6 17 C6
Marshall St. ST6 17 C4
May Av. ST6 17 C2
Mayfair Gdns. ST6 17 A2
Medway Walk. ST6 17 D1
Melfont St. ST6 17 C3
Melstone Av. ST6 17 C2
Metcalf Rd. ST6 17 D2
Mier St. ST6 17 B1
Mill Hayes Rd. ST6 17 B4
Mill Hill Cres. ST6 17 D1
Mitchell St. ST6 17 C4
Moorland Rd. ST6 17 D5
Mott Pl. ST6 17 B6
Mountford St. ST6 17 D5
Mousley St. ST6 17 B6
Murhall St. ST6 17 C5
Nash Peake St. ST6 17 A2
Navigation Rd. ST6 17 C6
Nephew St. ST6 17 B6
New Hayes Rd. ST6 17 B1
New St. ST6 17 C5
Newcastle St. ST6 17 A6
Newport La. ST6 17 B6
Newport St. ST6 17 B6
Nicholas St. ST6 17 D5
Nile St. ST6 17 D6
Norman Av. ST6 17 D2
Norris Rd. ST6 17 D2
Norton Av. ST6 17 D2
Odell Gro. ST6 17 B4
Old Court St. ST6 17 A2
Orme St. ST6 17 B6
Overhouse St. ST6 17 D5
Owen Gro. ST6 17 D5
Packhorse La. ST6 17 C6
Padlowe St. ST6 17 B5
Paradise St. ST6 17 A2
Parsonage St. ST6 17 A1
Persia Walk. ST6 17 A2
Phoenix St. ST6 17 A2
Piccadilly St. ST6 17 A2
Pierce St. ST6 17 A2
Pinnox St. ST6 17 B3
Pitcairn St. ST6 17 B2
Pitt St East. ST6 17 D6
Plex Street. ST6 17 A2
Port Vale Ct. ST6 17 D5
Port Vale St. ST6 17 B6
Price St. ST6 17 D5
Princess Sq. ST6 17 A6
Princess St. ST6 17 A3
Queen St. ST6 17 C6
Queens Av. ST6 17 C2
Railway St. ST6 17 B3
Rathbone St. ST6 17 B2
Regent Av. ST6 17 C2
Reginald St. ST6 17 D5
Reynolds Rd. ST6 17 D2
Richards Av. ST6 17 C2
Riley St Nth. ST6 17 C6
Riley St Sth. ST6 17 C6
Robert St. ST6 17 A1
Robin Croft. ST6 17 D6
Roundwell St. ST6 17 A2
Roylance St. ST6 17 A2
St Aidens St. ST6 17 A1
St Chads Rd. ST6 17 C2
St Johns Sq. ST6 17 C6
St Pauls St. ST6 17 B6
Salisbury St. ST6 17 B1
Sandra Clo. ST6 17 D3
Sant St. ST6 17 B6
Scotia La. ST6 17 C3
Scotia Rd. ST6 17 B2
Scott Lidgett Rd. ST6 17 A6
Sherwin Rd. ST6 17 D2
Shirley St. ST6 17 B6
Spens St. ST6 17 C6
Stanley St. ST6 17 B1
Station St. ST6 17 A6
Steventon Pl. ST6 17 C6
Stirling St. ST6 17 D6
Stringer Ct. ST6 17 A2
Stubbs St. ST6 17 B6
Summerbank Rd. ST6 17 A1
Sunnyside Av. ST6 17 C2
Swan Sq. ST6 17 D6
The Boulevard. ST6 17 B2
Thornley Rd. ST6 17 D2
Tomlinson St. ST6 17 A6
Tower St. ST6 17 A2
Tried St. ST6 17 B6
Trubshawe St. ST6 17 A6
Tyler Gro. ST6 17 C6
Ullswater Av. ST6 17 B5
Victoria Park Rd. ST6 17 B2
Wain St. ST6 17 D4
Walker St. ST6 17 B3
Wardle St. ST6 17 B2
Washington St. ST6 17 B3
Watergate St. ST6 17 A2
Waterloo Rd. ST6 17 D6
Waveney Walk Nth. ST6 17 D1
Waveney Walk Sth. ST6 17 D1
Wedgwood Pl. ST6 17 D5
Wedgwood St. ST6 17 D5
Wesley St. ST6 17 B2
Westport Rd. ST6 17 B3
Wilkinson St. ST6 17 B3
Wilks St. ST6 17 B1
William Clowes St. ST6 17 C6
Williamson St. ST6 17 B3
Woodbank St. ST6 17 C6
Woodland St. ST6 17 B2
Wycliffe St. ST6 17 C6
Yale St. ST6 17 B6
Zion St. ST6 17 D6

BURTON-UPON-TRENT

Abbey St. DE14 21 G6
Addie Rd. DE13 20 D1
Albert St. DE14 21 E3
Albion Ter. DE14 21 G1
Alfred St. DE14 21 F5
All Saints Rd. DE14 21 E6
Alma St. DE14 21 E6
Anglesey Rd. DE14 21 E6
Anson Ct. DE14 21 G4
Arthur St. DE14 21 F2
Ash St. DE14 21 E6
Ashby Rd. DE15 21 H4
Ashford Rd. DE13 20 A1
Astill St. DE15 21 H6
Balfour St. DE14 21 E1
Barley Clo. DE14 21 G1
Bearwood Hill Rd. DE15 21 H4
Becket Clo. DE14 21 E1
Beech St. DE14 21 E6
Belvedere Rd. DE13 20 A1
Belvoir Clo. DE13 20 D2
Belvoir Rd. DE13 20 D2
Blackpool St. DE14 21 F6
Blythefield. DE14 21 G3
Bond St. DE14 21 F6
Borough Rd. DE14 21 E4
Bosworth Dri. DE13 20 D1
Bradmore Rd. DE14 21 E2
Branston Rd. DE14 21 F6
Brizlingcote St. DE15 21 H6
Broadway St. DE14 21 E6
Brook St. DE14 21 F4
Burton Bridge. DE14 21 H4
Burton By-Pass. DE14 20 B6
Butler Ct. DE14 20 D4
Byrkley St. DE14 21 E3
Calais Rd. DE13 20 D1
Cambridge St. DE14 20 D6
Canal St. DE14 21 E5
Carlton St. DE13 21 E1
Carver Rd. DE14 21 E2
Casey La. DE14 21 E3
Chaucer Clo. DE14 21 F1
Clarence St. DE14 21 E6
Clay St. DE15 21 H6
Craven St. DE13 21 E1
Cross St. DE14 21 F5
Crossman St. DE14 20 C4
Curtis Way. DE14 20 D3
Curzon St. DE14 21 E4
Curzon St West. DE14 21 E4
Dale St. DE14 21 E5
Dallow Clo. DE14 21 E2
Dallow Cres. DE14 21 E2
Dallow St. DE14 21 E2
Dame Paulet Clo. DE14 21 G5
Denton Rd. DE13 20 C1
Derby Rd. DE14 21 F2
Derby St. DE14 21 E4
Derby St East. DE14 21 F3
Derwent Clo. DE14 21 H4
Dickens Clo. DE14 21 F1
Duke St. DE14 21 F5
Eaton Rd. DE14 21 G1
Edward St. DE14 21 E3
Electric St. DE14 21 G2
Elms Rd. DE15 21 H5
Elton Rd. DE14 21 F1
Eton Clo. DE14 21 G1
Evershed Way. DE14 21 E5
Falcon Clo. DE14 21 G2
Faversham Rd. DE13 20 C1
Fennel Wk. DE14 21 F5
Field La. DE13 20 C1
Flatts Clo. DE13 21 E1
Fleet St. DE14 21 F6
Forest Rd. DE13 20 A3
Foston Av. DE13 20 D1
Friars Wk. DE14 21 G5
George St. DE14 21 F4
Glensyl Way. DE14 21 G3
Goodman St. DE14 21 F2
Gordon St. DE14 21 E3
Gough Side. DE14 21 F5
Grain Warehouse Yd. DE14 21 E4
Grange Clo. DE14 21 E3
Grange St. DE14 20 D4
Green St. DE14 21 F6
Guild St. DE14 21 F4
Halcyon Ct. DE14 20 D3
Halcyon Way. DE14 20 D3
Harbury St. DE13 20 D1
Harlaxton St. DE13 20 D1
Hawkins La. DE14 21 F3
Hay Wk. DE14 21 G5
Henhurst Farm. DE13 20 A2
High St. DE14 21 G5
Highcroft Dri. DE14 20 C3
Horninglow Rd. DE14 21 F1
Horninglow Rd Nth. DE14 21 E1
Horninglow St. DE14 21 F3
Hunter St. DE14 21 F2
Ibstock St. DE13 20 D1

INDUSTRIAL & RETAIL:

Anderstaff Ind Est. DE14 21 G2
Burton Enterprise Park. DE14 21 G2
Clarke Ind Est. DE14 21 G3
Electric St Ind Est. DE14 21 H2
Falcon Business Centre. DE14 21 G2
Faycross Ind Est. DE14 21 G2
Femwork Ind Est. DE14 21 G2
Hawkins La Ind Est. DE14 21 G3
HCM Ind Est. DE14 21 G3
Ryknild Ind Trading Est. DE14 21 G1
Trent Ind Est. DE14 21 G3
Wharf Rd Ind Est. DE14 21 C
Windsor Ind Est. DE14 21 C
Yeoman Ind Est. DE14 21 C
*James Ct, James St. DE14 21
James St. DE14 21
Jennings Way. DE14 20
King Edward Pl. DE14 21
King St. DE14 21
Kingsley Rd. DE14 21
Lansdowne Ter. DE14 21
Lichfield St. DE14 21
Little Burton East. DE14 21
Little Burton West. DE14 21
Longmead Rd. DE14 21
Lordswell Rd. DE14 20
Lower Outwoods Rd. DE14 20
Lyndham Av. DE15 21 H
Lyne Ct. DE14 20 D
Malvern St. DE15 21 H
Manor Croft. DE14 21 G
Market Pl. DE14 21 G
Masefield Cres. DE14 21 F
Meadow Rd. DE14 21 H
Meadowside Dri. DE14 21 G
Meredith Clo. DE14 21 F
Millers La. DE14 21 E
Milton St. DE14 21 F
Mona Rd. DE14 20 D
Moor St. DE14 21 E
Moores Clo. DE14 21 E
Mosley St. DE14 21 E
Napier St. DE14 21 E
Needwood St. DE14 21 E
New St. DE14 21
Newton Mews. DE15 21 H
Newton Rd. DE15 21 H
Nicholson Way. DE14 20 D
Norton Rd. DE13 20 D
Oadby Rise. DE13 20 D
Oak St. DE14 21 E
Orchard Pk. DE14 21 F
Orchard St. DE14 21 F
Ordish Ct. DE14 21 F
Ordish St. DE14 21 F
Osbourne Ct. DE13 20 D
Outwoods La. DE13 20 A
Outwoods St. DE13 20 D
Oxford St. DE14 20 D
Paget St. DE14 21 E
Park St. DE14 21 F
Parker St. DE14 21 F
Parkway. DE14 20 E
Patch Clo. DE13 21 E
Peel St. DE14 21 E
Pensgreave Rd. DE13 21 E
Price Ct. DE14 20 C
Princess St. DE14 21 E
Princess Way. DE14 21 G
Queen St. DE14 21 E
Rangemore St. DE14 21 E
Ravens Way. DE14 20 D
Reservoir Rd. DE14 20 B
Richmond St. DE14 21 E
Rose Cottage Clo. DE14 21 F
Rose Cotaget Gdns. DE14 21 F
Rowton St. DE13 21 E
Ruskin Pl. DE14 21 F
Russell St. DE14 21 F
St Georges Rd. DE13 20 C
St Margarets. DE13 20 C
St Modwens Wk. DE14 21 G
St Pauls Ct. DE14 21 E
St Pauls Sq. DE14 21 E
St Pauls St West. DE14 20 D
St Peters Bridge. DE14 21 F
St Peters Ct. DE15 21 H
Scalpcliffe Rise. DE15 21 H
Scalpcliffe Rd. DE15 21 H
Second Av. DE14 20 B
Severn Dri. DE14 21 G
Shakespeare Rd. DE14 21 F
Shannon App.DE14 21 F
Sheffield St. DE14 21 F
Shelley Av. DE14 21 G
Shelley Clo. DE14 21 G
Shobnall Clo. DE14 21 E
Shobnall Rd. DE14 20 B
Shobnall St. DE14 20 D
Sinai Clo. DE14 20 B
Spring Terrace Rd. DE15 21 H
Stafford St. DE14 21 F
Stanley St. DE14 21 E
Stapenhill Rd. DE15 21 H

ation St. DE14 21 F4
van Ct. DE15 21 H4
van Wk. DE14 21 G5
vannington St. DE13 20 D1
dney St. DE14 21 F1
e Carousels. DE14 21 E2
e Cloisters. DE15 21 H6
e Grange. DE14 20 D4
e Maltings. DE14 21 G3
ird Av. DE14 20 B6
ornley St. DE14 21 F1
rent Ter,
Burton Bri. DE14 21 G4
nderhill Wk. DE14 21 F5
nion St. DE14 21 F5
kbridge St. DE14 21 E6
rnon Ter. DE14 21 E3
ctoria Cres. DE14 21 E2
ctoria Rd. DE14 21 F3
ctoria St. DE14 21 E3
alker St. DE14 21 E6
arwick St. DE14 21 E1
aterloo St. DE14 21 E3
atson St. DE14 21 F6
averley La. DE14 20 D4
elford Rise. DE13 20 C1
ellington Rd. DE14 20 C6
ellington St. DE14 21 E4
ellington St East.
DE14 21 E4
ellington St West.
DE14 21 E4
estfield Rd. DE13 21 E1
etmore La. DE14 21 H1
etmore Rd. DE14 21 G1
harf Rd. DE14 21 G2
heatbreach Clo. DE14 21 E2
illiam St. DE14 21 F2
ood Ct. DE14 21 F6
ood St. DE14 21 E6
ordsworth Clo. DE14 21 F1
orthington Wk. DE14 21 G5
orthington Way. DE14 21 G5
yggeston St. DE13 21 E1
ork St. DE14 21 E3

CANNOCK

dam Ct. WS11 22 C1
damson Clo. WS11 22 A1
lport Rd. WS11 22 D1
lport St. WS11 22 D1
ton Gro. WS11 22 A2
scot Dri. WS11 22 A3
von Rd. WS11 22 B3
ack Crofts. WS11 22 D2
anbury Rd. WS11 22 B2
arnswood Clo. WS11 22 A2
eau Ct. WS11 22 E1
eech Tree La. WS11 22 C2
eecroft Ct. WS11 22 D1
eecroft Rd. WS11 22 D1
elmont Av. WS11 22 B1
erwick Dri. WS11 22 B3
deford Way. WS11 22 A3
rch Av. WS11 22 B2
oyden Clo. WS11 22 A1
rook Vale. WS11 22 E3
rookfield Dri. WS11 22 D4
runswick Rd. WS11 22 D1
urnham Grn. WS11 22 A2
alving Hill. WS11 22 D1
anford Pl. WS11 22 E2
arfax. WS11 22 D3
arlisle Rd. WS11 22 A3
Caxton Ct,
Caxton St. WS11 22 D2
axton St. WS11 22 D2
halfont Av. WS11 22 B3
haseley Av. WS11 22 B1
haseley Croft. WS11 22 B1
hurch St. WS11 22 D2
lifton Av. WS11 22 B3
oniston Way. WS11 22 D2
onvent Clo. WS11 22 D3
onway Rd. WS11 22 A3
oppice Ct. WS11 22 B3
Cranford Pl,
Hednesford Rd. WS11 22 D2
anilo Rd. WS11 22 C2
artmouth Av. WS11 22 B3
artmouth Rd. WS11 22 C2
ee Gro. WS11 22 C3
elta Way. WS11 22 C4
erwent Gro. WS11 22 C3
evon Grn. WS11 22 E3
evon Rd. WS11 22 E2
on Gro. WS11 22 C3
orchester Rd. WS11 22 A2
Downesway. WS11 22 B1
Durnsley Dri. WS11 22 A1
Eastern Way. WS11 22 E4
Ellesmere Rd. WS11 22 A3
Ellis Walk. WS11 22 E3
*Elm Croft,
Church St. WS11 22 D2
Elms Dri. WS11 22 B2
Exeter Rd. WS11 22 A2
Fairway. WS11 22 C4
Falcon Clo. WS11 22 B1
Farmount Dri. WS11 22 D2
Fern Dell Clo. WS11 22 B1
Filey Clo. WS11 22 B3
Forrest Av. WS11 22 D3
Girton Rd. WS11 22 D3
Goldthorne Av. WS11 22 E1
Gorsey La. WS11 22 B2
Gowland Dri. WS11 22 A1
Grainger Ct.WS11 22 D1
Grange Dri. WS11 22 E1
Greenfields. WS11 22 E1
Hall Ct Clo. WS11 22 D2
Hall Ct Cres. WS11 22 D2
Hall Ct La. WS11 22 D2
Hampton Grn. WS11 22 D3
Hampton St. WS11 22 C3
Hannaford Way. WS11 22 E1
Harrison Rd. WS11 22 D3
Hatherton Croft. WS11 22 B1
Hatherton Rd. WS11 22 A2
Hatton Rd. WS11 22 A2
Hawks Green La. WS11 22 F1
Hawksville Dri. WS11 22 E1
Hayes Way. WS11 22 F2
Hazelwood Gro. WS11 22 C2
Hazlemere Gro. WS11 22 A3
Hednesford Rd. WS11 22 D2
Hednesford St. WS11 22 E2
High Bank. WS11 22 D3
High Green. WS11 22 C2
Holder Dri. WS11 22 A1
Hollies Av. WS11 22 E2
Hunter Rd. WS11 22 D2
INDUSTRIAL & RETAIL:
Avon Business Park.
WS11 22 B4
Cedars Business Centre.
WS11 22 B3
Chase Centre. WS11 22 D2
Hollies Business Centre.
WS11 22 E2
Linkway Retail Park.
WS11 22 A4
Martindale Ind Est.
WS11 22 F1
Mill Park Ind Est.
WS11 22 F1
Orbital Centre. WS11 22 E4
Progress Business Pk.
WS11 22 E4
Rumer Hill
Business Est. WS11 22 E3
Virage Park. WS11 22 E4
Ivy Clo. WS11 22 C3
Keeble Clo. WS11 22 D3
Keeling Dri. WS11 22 A1
Kendal Ct. WS11 22 A3
*Kenilworth Ct,
New St. WS11 22 E2
Kilmorie Rd. WS11 22 B1
*Kingston Arc,
Walsall Rd. WS11 22 D2
Kingswood Av. WS11 22 B3
Laburnum Av. WS11 22 C4
Laburnum Clo. WS11 22 D3
Langdale Dri. WS11 22 B3
Langdale Grn. WS11 22 B3
Leamington Clo. WS11 22 B3
Lichfield Rd. WS11 22 E2
Lilac Av. WS11 22 C4
Lincoln Dri. WS11 22 E3
Lloyd St. WS11 22 C2
*Longford Ct,
Bideford Way. WS11 22 A2
Longford Grn. WS11 22 B3
Longford Rd. WS11 22 A1
Manor Av. WS11 22 C2
Maple Cres. WS11 22 B2
Market Hall St. WS11 22 D2
Market Pl. WS11 22 D2
Marshwood Clo. WS11 22 F1
Martindale. WS11 22 F1
Melchester Wk. WS11 22 E1
Meriden Clo. WS11 22 A2
Merlin Clo. WS11 22 B1
Mill Park. WS11 22 F1
Mill St. WS11 22 D2
Millbrook Clo. WS11 22 F1
Mosswood St. WS11 22 C3
New Penkridge Rd.
WS11 22 A1
New St. WS11 22 D4
New St. WS11 22 E2
Newhall St. WS11 22 C2
Nirvana Clo. WS11 22 B1
North St. WS11 22 D4
Oaks Dri. WS11 22 B2
Oakwoods. WS11 22 C3
Old Hednesford Rd.
WS11 22 E1
Old Penkridge Rd.
WS11 22 B1
Orbital Way. WS11 22 E4
Orchard Av. WS11 22 B1
Oriel Clo. WS11 22 D3
Oxford Grn. WS11 22 F3
Oxford Rd. WS11 22 F3
Park Rd. WS11 22 C1
Park St. WS11 22 D4
Parkside La. WS11 22 A1
Pebblemill Clo. WS11 22 E1
Pebblemill Dri. WS11 22 E1
Pennine Dri. WS11 22 D1
Poplar La. WS11 22 A2
Portland Pl. WS11 22 B3
Price St. WS11 22 D2
Progress Dri. WS11 22 D4
Pye Green Rd. WS11 22 D1
Queen St. WS11 22 C2
Queens Sq. WS11 22 D2
Railway St. WS11 22 E2
Reamington Dri. WS11 22 E2
Repton Clo. WS11 22 B3
Ridings Brook Dri. WS11 22 F1
Ringway. WS11 22 D2
Rockholt Cres. WS11 22 B1
*Rowan Ct,
Ringway. WS11 22 D2
Rowan Rd. WS11 22 B1
Rumer Hill Rd. WS11 22 E3
St James Rd. WS11 22 B2
St Johns Clo. WS11 22 C3
St Johns Rd. WS11 22 C3
St Lukes Clo. WS11 22 C2
Salcombe Clo. WS11 22 B3
Salop Dri. WS11 22 E3
Sandy La. WS11 22 A1
Sherbrook Rd. WS11 22 B1
Shoal Hill Clo. WS11 22 B1
Skipton Pl. WS11 22 A3
South Clo. WS11 22 B3
Southgate End. WS11 22 B3
Spinney Farm Rd.
WS11 22 A3
Spring St. WS11 22 E3
Stafford Rd. WS11 22 C1
Stirling Pl. WS11 22 A3
Stoney Croft. WS11 22 E1
Stoney Lea Rd. WS11 22 E1
Stoneyfields Clo. WS11 22 F1
Strathmore Pl. WS11 22 E1
Sunfield Rd. WS11 22 A2
Surrey Clo. WS11 22 E2
Tame Gro. WS11 22 C3
The Glade. WS11 22 B1
The Green. WS11 22 D2
The Willows. WS11 22 B2
Thirlmere Clo. WS11 22 E1
Trinity Clo. WS11 22 D3
Ullswater Rd. WS11 22 D1
Victoria St. WS11 22 C2
Walhouse St. WS11 22 D3
Walsall Rd. WS11 22 D2
Warwick Clo. WS11 22 E2
Watling St. WS11 22 A4
Waveney Gro. WS11 22 A2
Wellfield Clo. WS11 22 A3
Wellington Dri. WS11 22 A2
Wessex Dri. WS11 22 E1
Whinyates Rise. WS11 22 E3
Whitby Way. WS11 22 B3
Windermere Pl. WS11 22 D1
Wolverhampton Rd.
WS11 22 A4
Wolverhampton Rd.
WS11 22 C3
Wootton Ct.WS11 22 E1
Worcester Clo. WS11 22 E3
York Rd. WS11 22 E3

CHEADLE

Alexandre Palace. ST10 23 C3
Allen St. ST10 23 C4
Arundel Dri. ST10 23 C4
Ash Clo. ST10 23 C4
Ashbourne Rd. ST10 23 C4
Ashtree Hill. ST10 23 A4
Attlee Rd. ST10 23 B5
Austen Clo. ST10 23 A5
Avon Gro. ST10 23 C6
Aynslay Clo. ST10 23 A6
Ayr Rd. ST10 23 C2
Baddeley St. ST10 23 B4
Bala Gro. ST10 23 C2
Bank St. ST10 23 B4
Barleycroft. ST10 23 C5
Basset Clo. ST10 23 A4
Beech Clo. ST10 23 D4
Beswick Clo. ST10 23 B6
Bittern Clo. ST10 23 C4
Browning Clo. ST10 23 A5
Byron Clo. ST10 23 A5
Carlos Clo. ST10 23 A4
Carlton Clo. ST10 23 B6
Cecily Ter. ST10 23 C3
Cedar Clo. ST10 23 C4
Chapel St. ST10 23 B4
Charles St. ST10 23 B4
Chasewater Gro. ST10 23 D2
Cheltenham Av. ST10 23 C2
Cherry La. ST10 23 D1
Church St. ST10 23 B3
Churchill Rd. ST10 23 B2
Churnet Gro. ST10 23 C5
Coalfort Clo. ST10 23 A5
Coleridge Dri. ST10 23 A5
Coneygreave Clo. ST10 23 B6
Coniston Dri. ST10 23 C2
Conway Gro. ST10 23 C6
Copeland Clo. ST10 23 B5
Croft Rd. ST10 23 B3
Cross St. ST10 23 B3
Croxden Clo. ST10 23 B6
Dale Clo. ST10 23 C4
Dandillion Av. ST10 23 B6
Dane Gro. ST10 23 C6
Dart Gro. ST10 23 C6
Derwent Dri. ST10 23 C6
Donkey La. ST10 23 B1
Doulton Clo. ST10 23 B6
Dovedale Clo. ST10 23 C1
Draycott Dri. ST10 23 B6
Dryden Way. ST10 23 A5
Eaves La. ST10 23 B6
Eden Gro. ST10 23 C6
Elm Dri. ST10 23 C4
Epsom Clo. ST10 23 C2
Foxfield Clo. ST10 23 C1
Friars Clo. ST10 23 B3
*Friars Ct,
Croft Rd. ST10 23 B3
Froghall Rd. ST10 23 B2
Giles Clo. ST10 23 B4
Glebe Clo. ST10 23 A4
Glebe Rd. ST10 23 A4
Goodwood Av. ST10 23 C3
Graitham Gro. ST10 23 D2
Greenfield Cres. ST10 23 B2
Greenways Dri. ST10 23 B2
Hammersley Hayes Rd.
ST10 23 C1
Harbourne Ct. ST10 23 B3
Harbourne Rd. ST10 23 B3
Hardy Clo. ST10 23 A5
Harewood Clo. ST10 23 B2
Hawfinch Rd. ST10 23 C4
Haydock Clo. ST10 23 C2
Hayes Hall Rd. ST10 23 C3
High St. ST10 23 B3
Highfield Av. ST10 23 B2
Highfield Clo. ST10 23 B2
Huntley Clo. ST10 23 B6
INDUSTRIAL & RETAIL:
Harewood
Ind Est. ST10 23 A2
Keeling Rd. ST10 23 C3
Kempton Gro. ST10 23 C2
Kestrel La. ST10 23 C4
Kingfisher Cres. ST10 23 C4
Leek Rd. ST10 23 A1
Lid La. ST10 23 A4
Litley Dri. ST10 23 B6
Lommond Gro. ST10 23 C2
Mackenzie Cres. ST10 23 B5
Majors Barn. ST10 23 A4
Mallory Way. ST10 23 C3
Manifold Dri. ST10 23 C6
Mansion Clo. ST10 23 C5
Maple Clo. ST10 23 C4
Masefield Clo. ST10 23 B2
Meadow Dri. ST10 23 B4
Meakin Clo. ST10 23 A5
Mill Gro. ST10 23 C5
Millbrook Way. ST10 23 C5
Millers View. ST10 23 C5
Millhouse Dri. ST10 23 C5
Mills Rd. ST10 23 B4
Millstream Clo. ST10 23 C5
Millwaters. ST10 23 C5
Minton Clo. ST10 23 B5
Monkhouse. ST10 23 B3
Moor La. ST10 23 C3
Moorcroft Clo. ST10 23 A5
Moorland Walk. ST10 23 B3
Moss La. ST10 23 D6
Ness Gro. ST10 23 C2
Newmarket Way. ST10 23 C2
Nursery Clo. ST10 23 A3
Oak St. ST10 23 B4
Oulton Rd. ST10 23 C3
Paragon Clo. ST10 23 A5
Park Av. ST10 23 B5
Park Dri. ST10 23 A2
Park La. ST10 23 A3
Park La Clo. ST10 23 A4
Park Ter. ST10 23 B4
Plant St. ST10 23 B4
Prince George St. ST10 23 B3
Pullman Ct. ST10 23 A5
Queen St. ST10 23 B3
Rawle Clo. ST10 23 A4
Rakeway Rd. ST10 23 C5
Robina Dri. ST10 23 C3
Rockingham Dri. ST10 23 D4
Royal Wk. ST10 23 B4
Rudyard Way. ST10 23 C3
Sandown Clo. ST10 23 C1
Shelley Dri. ST10 23 A5
Shelsley Rd. ST10 23 C3
Silverstone Av. ST10 23 C3
Spode Clo. ST10 23 A5
Stanfield Cres. ST10 23 B6
Station Rd. ST10 23 B5
Stokesay Dri. ST10 23 D4
Sun St. ST10 23 C3
Sunwell Gdns. ST10 23 C4
Tamar Gro. ST10 23 C6
Tape St. ST10 23 B3
Tay Clo. ST10 23 C2
Tean Rd. ST10 23 B6
Tennyson Clo. ST10 23 A5
Thames Dri. ST10 23 C6
The Avenue. ST10 23 B4
The Birches. ST10 23 B4
The Bramshaws. ST10 23 C4
The Green. ST10 23 A4
The Paddock. ST10 23 B5
The Sidings. ST10 23 B5
The Terrace. ST10 23 B4
Thorley Dri. ST10 23 C4
Thorpe Rise. ST10 23 C1
Town End. ST10 23 A4
Trent Clo. ST10 23 C6
Tuscan Clo. ST10 23 A5
Ullswater Dri. ST10 23 C3
Victory Cres. ST10 23 B2
Wade Clo. ST10 23 B5
Watt Pl. ST10 23 B4
Weaver Clo. ST10 23 C1
Wedgwood Rd. ST10 23 A5
Well St. ST10 23 B3
Wetherby Clo. ST10 23 C2
Windermere Av. ST10 23 C2
Windy Arbour. ST10 23 B3
Woodhead Yd. ST10 23 B1
Wordsworth Clo. ST10 23 A5
Young St. ST10 23 C4

CHEDDLETON

Ashcombe Rd. ST13 24 B6
Basford La. ST13 24 D1
Basford Vw. ST13 24 B4
Basfordbridge La. ST13 24 B6
Beech Av. ST13 24 B6
Botham Dri. ST13 24 B5
Boucher Rd. ST13 24 A6
Brindley Cres. ST13 24 B6
Brittain Av. ST13 24 C5
Brooklands Way. ST13 24 D1
Burgis Av. ST13 24 B6
Cauldon Av. ST13 24 C5
Cheadle Rd. ST13 24 A6
Cheadle Rd. ST13 24 C3
Cheddleton Heath Rd.
ST13 24 C3
Cheddleton Park Av.
ST13 24 C5
Cheddleton Rd. ST13 24 D1
Churchill Av. ST13 24 B6
Churnet Clo. ST13 24 A6
Crony Clo. ST13 24 A6
Dalehouse Rd. ST13 24 A6
East Dri. ST13 24 B3
Grange Rd. ST13 24 B6
Grangefields Clo. ST13 24 B6
Haig Clo. ST13 24 C5

Harrison Way. ST13 — 24 C4
Hazelhurst Dri. ST13 — 24 B5
Heathview. ST13 — 24 C3
High La. ST13 — 24 C3
Hillside Rd. ST13 — 24 A6
Hollow La. ST13 — 24 A5
Holly Av. ST13 — 24 B6
INDUSTRIAL & RETAIL:
Churnetside
Business Pk. ST13 — 24 B4
Leekbrook Ind Est.
ST13 — 24 C1
Kingsley View. ST13 — 24 C5
Leek Rd. ST13 — 24 B4
Leekbrook Way. ST13 — 24 D1
Moorland. ST13 — 24 B5
Moridge Vw. ST13 — 24 B6
Oak Av. ST13 — 24 B6
Ostlers La. ST13 — 24 A6
Ox Pasture. ST13 — 24 A5
Park La. ST13 — 24 A4
Rennie Cres. ST13 — 24 B5
St Edwards Rd. ST13 — 24 A6
St Hildas Av. ST13 — 24 A6
Shaffalong La. ST13 — 24 A5
Sneyd Clo. ST13 — 24 B4
Station Rd. ST13 — 24 B4
Steele Clo. ST13 — 24 C5
The Avenue. ST13 — 24 B6
The Croft. ST13 — 24 B6
The Roche. ST13 — 24 B6
Villa Rd. ST13 — 24 A3
Wall La Ter. ST13 — 24 A3
West Dri. ST13 — 24 A3
Westwood Clo. ST13 — 24 A6

CHESLYN HAY/ GREAT WYRLEY

Achilles Clo. WS6 — 25 C5
Acorn Clo. WS6 — 25 D5
Ajax Clo. WS6 — 25 C6
Alpha Way. WS6 — 25 D6
Alwyn Clo. WS6 — 25 C3
Anson Clo. WS6 — 25 C5
Anson Rd. WS6 — 25 C5
Anstree Clo. WS6 — 25 A5
Appledore Clo. WS6 — 25 D3
Ash La. WS6 — 25 D3
Barn Croft. WS6 — 25 D3
Beaumont Clo. WS6 — 25 C4
Beaumont Dri. WS6 — 25 C4
Beech Ct. WS11 — 25 D2
Belmont Clo. WS11 — 25 D2
Bentons La. WS6 — 25 D5
Berwyn Gro. WS6 — 25 C4
Bluebell La. WS6 — 25 D6
Boleyn Clo. WS6 — 25 A5
Bramwell Dri. WS6 — 25 A6
Bratch Hollow. WS6 — 25 D1
Bridge Av. WS6 — 25 B2
Bridge St. WS11 — 25 B1
Broad Meadow La.
WS6 — 25 D5
Broad St. WS11 — 25 B1
Brook La. WS6 — 25 D4
Brook Rd. WS6 — 25 B2
Brooklands Av. WS6 — 25 C2
Campians Av. WS6 — 25 A4
Cedar Gro. WS6 — 25 D2
Chapel Sq. WS6 — 25 B3
Collier Clo. WS6 — 25 A4
Charles Clo. WS6 — 25 A5
Chase Av. WS6 — 25 C4
Cherrington Clo. WS6 — 25 C2
Cheslyn Dri. WS6 — 25 A4
Chestnut Dri. WS6 — 25 A3
Chestnut Clo. WS6 — 25 C4
Chillington Clo. WS6 — 25 C6
Chilton Clo. WS6 — 25 A6
Cleves Cres. WS6 — 25 A5
Clover Ridge. WS6 — 25 A4
Coltsfoot Vw. WS6 — 25 B4
Coppice Clo. WS6 — 25 B3
Coppice La. WS6 — 25 A2
Cotswold Av. WS6 — 25 C3
Cranmer Clo. WS6 — 25 A5
Cromwell Ct. WS6 — 25 D5
Cross St,
Cheslyn Hay. WS6 — 25 A4
Cross St,
Churchbridge. WS11 — 25 B1
Darges La. WS6 — 25 C2
Deanfield Dri. WS6 — 25 C3
Dove Hollow. WS6 — 25 C5
Dundalk La. WS6 — 25 A5
Dunston Clo. WS6 — 25 B6
Eagle Clo. WS6 — 25 A4
Eastern La. WS11 — 25 C1

Estridge La. WS6 — 25 D4
Fair Oaks Dri. WS6 — 25 D6
Fairview Clo. WS6 — 25 A4
Falcon Clo. WS6 — 25 A4
Fennel Clo. WS6 — 25 B3
Field La. WS6 — 25 C4
Forest Glade. WS6 — 25 C4
Forest Way. WS6 — 25 D5
Foxland Av. WS6 — 25 D3
Frensham Clo. WS6 — 25 B3
Gemini Dri. WS11 — 25 C1
Gilpins Croft. WS6 — 25 A5
Glenthorne Dri. WS6 — 25 B4
Gorsey La. WS6 — 25 C6
Grassmere Ct. WS6 — 25 A4
Green La. WA11 — 25 C1
Hall La. WS6 — 25 C3
Harrison Clo. WS6 — 25 D4
Hartwell La. WS6 — 25 D4
Hatherton St. WS6 — 25 A4
Hawkins Dri. WS11 — 25 A2
Hawks Clo. WS6 — 25 A5
Hawthorn Av. WS6 — 25 D5
Hawthorne Rd. WS6 — 25 B2
Hayes View Dri. WS6 — 25 B2
Hazel La. WS6 — 25 D4
Hazelwood Clo. WS6 — 25 B4
High St. WS6 — 25 A4
Highfields Grange. WS6 — 25 A6
Highfields Park. WS6 — 25 A6
Hilton La. WS6 — 25 D5
Holly La. WS6 — 25 B6
Honeysuckle Way. WS6 — 25 D2
Hornegate Ho. WS6 — 25 D2
Hut Hill La. WS6 — 25 D2
INDUSTRIAL & RETAIL:
Cannock Ind Centre.
WS11 — 25 A1
Field Trading Est.
WS11 — 25 A1
Green Lane Venture
Centre. WS11 — 25 C1
Landywood
Enterprise Pk. WS6 — 25 C6
Orbital Retail Centre.
WS11 — 25 C1
Park Venture Centre.
WS11 — 25 B1
South Staffordshire
Business Pk. WS11 — 25 A2
The Exchange Ind Est.
WS11 — 25 B1
The Phoenix Centre.
WS11 — 25 B1
Walkmill Business
Park. WS11 — 25 A1
Wyrley Brook Pk.
WS11 — 25 A1
Jacobs Hall La. WS6 — 25 D6
Johns La. WS6 — 25 C4
Joness La. WS6 — 25 D5
Jubilee Clo. WS6 — 25 C5
Julian Clo. WS6 — 25 D3
Kempton Dri. WS6 — 25 C4
Kestrel Way. WS6 — 25 A5
Kingswood Dri. WS6 — 25 D2
Lambourne Clo. WS6 — 25 C4
Landywood Grn. WS6 — 25 B5
Landywood La. WS6 — 25 B4
Lapwing Clo. WS6 — 25 A5
Lea La. WS6 — 25 D4
Leacroft La. WS11 — 25 C2
Leander Clo. WS11 — 25 C5
Leveson Av. WS6 — 25 B4
Lilac Av. WS6 — 25 D6
Lime Clo. WS6 — 25 C2
Lingfield Clo. WS6 — 25 C4
Lingfield Dri. WS6 — 25 C4
Littlewood La. WS6 — 25 B2
Littlewood Rd. WS6 — 25 B3
Lodge La. WS11 — 25 A2
Love La. WS6 — 25 B4
Low St. WS6 — 25 A4
Magna Clo. WS6 — 25 B3
Manor Av. WS6 — 25 D3
March Clo. WS6 — 25 A5
Meadow Gro. WS6 — 25 D4
Merrill Clo. WS6 — 25 B5
Mill La. WS11 — 25 A2
Mitre Rd. WS6 — 25 A4
Moat La. WS6 — 25 D4
Moons La. WS6 — 25 A5
Mount Clo. WS6 — 25 B4
Mount Pleasant. WS6 — 25 B4
New Horse Rd. WS6 — 25 B4
New St. WS6 — 25 D5
Newbury Clo. WS6 — 25 C4
Norfolk Gr. WS6 — 25 C6
North St. WS11 — 25 B1
Norton La. WS6 — 25 D3
Nuthurst Rd. WS6 — 25 C2

Oak Av. WS6 — 25 D5
Oak Ho. WS6 — 25 D5
Oakdene Clo. WS6 — 25 A5
Oaken Grange. WS6 — 25 C5
Oakridge Dri. WS6 — 25 C4
Old Falls Clo. WS6 — 25 A4
Old Hall La. WS6 — 25 C3
Orbital Way. WS11 — 25 C1
Orchard Clo. WS6 — 25 B3
Orion Clo. WS6 — 25 C5
Oxford Clo. WS6 — 25 C3
Oxley Clo. WS6 — 25 C5
Paddock La. WS6 — 25 B3
Park Clo. WS6 — 25 B3
Park La. WS6 — 25 D3
Park St,
Cheslyn Hay. WS6 — 25 B3
Park St,
Churchbridge. WS11 — 25 B1
Peace Clo. WS6 — 25 D4
Pendrel Clo. WS6 — 25 C6
Penny Ct. WS6 — 25 D6
Pine Clo. WS6 — 25 C2
Pinfold Ho. WS6 — 25 A4
Pinfold La. WS6 — 25 A4
Plants Clo. WS6 — 25 D6
Pool Meadow. WS6 — 25 A5
Pool Vw. WS6 — 25 D2
Poplar Rd. WS6 — 25 B4
Quarry Clo. WS6 — 25 B4
Queen St. WS6 — 25 A4
Quinton Venue. WS6 — 25 C3
Ramillies Cres. WS6 — 25 C5
Raven Clo. WS6 — 25 A5
Robins Clo. WS6 — 25 A5
Roman Ct. WS11 — 25 B1
Roman Vw. WS11 — 25 B1
Rosemary Av. WS6 — 25 A4
Rosemary Rd. WS6 — 25 A3
Rosewood Pk. WS6 — 25 A5
St Marks Clo. WS6 — 25 C3
Sandown Av. WS6 — 25 B4
Saxon Clo. WS6 — 25 D5
Seymour Clo. WS6 — 25 A5
Shanklyn Clo. WS6 — 25 C3
Shaws La. WS6 — 25 D5
Short La. WS6 — 25 B4
Somerford Clo. WS6 — 25 B6
South Field Way. WS6 — 25 D4
Spring Dri. WS6 — 25 D4
Spring Meadow. WS6 — 25 A5
Station Rd. WS6 — 25 C2
Station St. WS6 — 25 B3
Streets La. WS6 — 25 B3
Sunbeam Dri. WS6 — 25 C3
Sunset Clo. WS6 — 25 C3
Sutherland Rd. WS6 — 25 B4
Swan Clo. WS6 — 25 A5
Telford Av. WS6 — 25 C4
Tenniscore Av. WS6 — 25 D4
The Crescent. WS6 — 25 D4
The Croft. WS6 — 25 C4
Thornley Croft. WS6 — 25 A6
Tower View Rd. WS6 — 25 C6
Trevor Av. WS6 — 25 D3
Triton Clo. WS6 — 25 C5
Tudor Clo. WS6 — 25 B3
Tudor Way. WS6 — 25 A5
Union St. WS11 — 25 B1
Upper Landywood La.
WS6 — 25 B5
Valley Grn. WS6 — 25 B4
Vine La. WS11 — 25 A1
Voyager Dri. WS11 — 25 C1
Walkmill La. WS11 — 25 A1
Walkmill Way. WS11 — 25 A1
Wallace Ct. WS6 — 25 A6
Walsall Rd,
Cannock. WS11 — 25 C1
Walsall Rd,
Gt Wyrley. WS6 — 25 D6
Wardles La. WS6 — 25 C4
Watling St. WS6 — 25 A1
Well La. WS6 — 25 D6
Wesley Av. WS6 — 25 A4
Westbourne Av. WS6 — 25 B3
Weston Dri. WS6 — 25 B6
Wharwell La. WS6 — 25 D5
Windsor Rd. WS6 — 25 B3
Woodgreen. WS6 — 25 B1
Woodland Dri. WS6 — 25 B2
Woodman La. WS6 — 25 B2
Woody Bank. WS6 — 25 C4
Yemscroft. WS6 — 25 D6
Zion Clo. WS6 — 25 A4

CODSALL

Acacia Cres. WV8 — 26 E2
Acorn Gro. WV8 — 26 B3

Albert Clo. WV8 — 26 B2
Alexander Rd. WV8 — 26 F2
Arps Rd. WV8 — 26 C2
Ash Clo. WV8 — 26 C2
Ashley Gdns. WV8 — 26 C2
Azalea Clo. WV8 — 26 E3
Bakers Gdns. WV8 — 26 B1
Bakers Way. WV8 — 26 B2
Beech Gdns. WV8 — 26 C4
Belvide Gdns. WV8 — 26 C1
Bentley Dri. WV8 — 26 C2
Bilbrook Ct. WV8 — 26 E2
Bilbrook Gro. WV8 — 26 E3
Bilbrook Rd. WV8 — 26 D2
Birches Av. WV8 — 26 F4
Birches Park Rd. WV8 — 26 D4
Birches Rd. WV8 — 26 E3
Blythe Gdns. WV8 — 26 C3
Broadway. WV8 — 26 C2
Bromley Gdns. WV8 — 26 C2
Brook Gro. WV8 — 26 E3
Brook Mdws. WV8 — 26 A1
Brookfield Rd. WV8 — 26 E1
Canford Cres. WV8 — 26 B2
Carter Av. WV8 — 26 E2
Cedar Gro. WV8 — 26 E2
Chadwell Gdns. WV8 — 26 C2
Chapel La. WV8 — 26 B2
Charters Av. WV8 — 26 E4
Cherry Tree Gdns. WV8 — 26 E2
Cherry Tree La. WV8 — 26 E2
Chestnut Clo. WV8 — 26 C3
Chillington Dri. WV8 — 26 D2
Chillington La. WV8 — 26 A1
Church Hill. WV8 — 26 C1
Church La. WV8 — 26 C1
Church Rd. WV8 — 26 C1
Clifton Gdns. WV8 — 26 F3
Codsall Gdns. WV8 — 26 B2
Cottage Vw. WV8 — 26 E2
Cranley Dri. WV8 — 26 C1
Crompton Ct. WV8 — 26 E1
Downie Rd. WV8 — 26 F3
Drury La. WV8 — 26 C1
Duck La. WV8 — 26 E3
Elliots La. WV8 — 26 D2
Elm Gro. WV8 — 26 D2
Fairfield Dri. WV8 — 26 B2
Farm Cres. WV8 — 26 C3
Farway Gdns. WV8 — 26 C3
Flemmynge Clo. WV8 — 26 B2
Florence Rd. WV8 — 26 F2
Forsythia Gro. WV8 — 26 D3
Glen Ct. WV8 — 26 D2
Gorsty Hayes. WV8 — 26 C2
Green Oak Rd. WV8 — 26 E3
Greenacre Dri. WV8 — 26 E4
Gunstone La. WV8 — 26 C1
Hawthorne La. WV8 — 26 C4
Heath Farm Rd. WV8 — 26 E3
Heath Gro. WV8 — 26 E3
Heath House La. WV8 — 26 B4
Histons Dri. WV8 — 26 C3
Histons Hill. WV8 — 26 C3
Hollybush La. WV8 — 26 A3
Holyhead Rd. WV8 — 26 A4
Homefield Rd. WV8 — 26 F2
Jasmine Gro. WV8 — 26 E3
Joeys La. WV8 — 26 F2
Keepers La. WV8 — 26 D3
Kingsley Gdns. WV8 — 26 B3
Kynaston Cres. WV8 — 26 E4
Lane Grn Av. WV8 — 26 F4
Lane Grn Ct. WV8 — 26 E3
Lane Grn Rd. WV8 — 26 E3
Lansdowne Av. WV8 — 26 B4
Lime Tree Gdns. WV8 — 26 E2
Lime Tree Rd. WV8 — 26 E2
Long Acre. WV8 — 26 C3
Loveridge Clo. WV8 — 26 C2
Madeira Av. WV8 — 26 D4
Magnolia Gro. WV8 — 26 E3
Malpass Gdns. WV8 — 26 B1
Manor Clo. WV8 — 26 E2
Manor Fold. WV8 — 26 A3
Manor House Pk. WV8 — 26 B2
Maybury Clo. WV8 — 26 B2
Meadow Vale. WV8 — 26 E4
Meadow Way. WV8 — 26 B3
Middle La. WV8 — 26 A3
Mill Gro. WV8 — 26 F2
Mill La. WV8 — 26 C3
Mill Stream Clo. WV8 — 26 E1
Millenium Way. WV8 — 26 F2
Moat Brook Av. WV8 — 26 B1
Moatbrook La. WV8 — 26 A1
Mount Gdns. WV8 — 26 C2
Nursery Gdns. WV8 — 26 C2
Oaken Covert. WV8 — 26 B3

Oaken Dri. WV8 — 26 A
Oaken Gro. WV8 — 26 B
Oaken La. WV8 — 26 A
Oaken Lanes. WV8 — 26 B
Oaken Pk. WV8 — 26 D
Oakfield Rd. WV8 — 26 B
Oakleigh Dri. WV8 — 26 D
Orchard La. WV8 — 26 B
Palmers Clo. WV8 — 26 F
Palmers Way. WV8 — 26 B
Parkes Av. WV8 — 26 B
Pendeford Hall La. WV8 — 26 B
Pendeford Mill La. WV8 — 26 B
Pendinas Dri. WV8 — 26 B
Pendrell Clo. WV8 — 26 D
Pine Wk. WV8 — 26 C
Poplars Dri. WV8 — 26 C
Primrose Gdns. WV8 — 26 D
Princes Clo. WV8 — 26 D
Princes Gdns. WV8 — 26 C
Queens Gdns. WV8 — 26 C
Ravenhill Dri. WV8 — 26 B
Red Rock Dri. WV8 — 26 B
Reeves Gdns. WV8 — 26 B
Ringhills Rd. WV8 — 26 B
Roseville Gdns. WV8 — 26 C
Sandy La. WV8 — 26 C
School Clo. WV8 — 26 C
Sherborne Gdns. WV8 — 26 D
Shop La. WV8 — 26 A
Slade Gdns. WV8 — 26 A
Slate La. WV8 — 26 A
South View Clo. WV8 — 26 F
Stafford La. WV8 — 26 A
Station Clo. WV8 — 26 C
Station Rd. WV8 — 26 B
Stoneleigh Gdns. WV8 — 26 C
Strawmoor La. WV8 — 26 A
Stretton Gdns. WV8 — 26 C
Suckling Green La.
WV8 — 26 C
The Drive. WV8 — 26 C
The Paddock. WV8 — 26 D
The Fields. WV8 — 26 E
The Woodlands. WV8 — 26 D
Vaughan Gdns. WV8 — 26 B
Walnut Av. WV8 — 26 E
Walton Gdns. WV8 — 26 C
Ward Rd. WV8 — 26 B
Warner Rd. WV8 — 26 C
Warwick Dri. WV8 — 26 B
Watery La. WV8 — 26 D
Watsons Gro. WV8 — 26 E
Wayside Acres. WV8 — 26 C
Wergs Hall Rd. WV8 — 26 C
Wesley Av. WV8 — 26 E
Wesley Rd. WV8 — 26 C
Wheel Av. WV8 — 26 C
Wheeler Clo. WV8 — 26 C
Wheelfields. WV8 — 26 C
Whitfield Clo. WV8 — 26 E
Wilkes Rd. WV8 — 26 E
Willow Dri. WV8 — 26 E
Windsor Gdns. WV8 — 26 B
Withers Rd. WV8 — 26 E
Wolverhampton Rd.
WV8 — 26 C
Wood Rd. WV8 — 26 A
Woodside Gro. WV8 — 26 E
Yew Tree Gdns. WV8 — 26 D

HANLEY

Acton St. ST1 — 27 D
Addison St. ST1 — 27 D
Adkins St. ST6 — 27 B
Adventure Pl. ST1 — 27 C
Albion Sq. ST1 — 27 C
Albion St. ST1 — 27 C
Arbour St. ST1 — 27 C
Armstrong Grn. ST6 — 27 C
Ashbourne Gro. ST1 — 27 C
Ashburton St. ST6 — 27 A
*Ashmore Wlk,
St Ann St. ST1 — 27 D
Avoca St. ST1 — 27 D
Bagnall St. ST1 — 27 D
Balfour St. ST1 — 27 B
Bamford Gro. ST1 — 27 B
Barrett Cres. ST6 — 27 A
Barrett Dri. ST6 — 27 A
Baskerville Rd. ST1 — 27 D
Beckford St. ST1 — 27 D
Bethell Rd. ST1 — 27 D
Bettany Rd. ST6 — 27 A
Bexley St. ST1 — 27 D
Birch Ter. ST1 — 27 D

ches Head Rd. ST1 27 D3
d Cage Walk. ST1 27 B6
kett St. ST1 27 B5
ck Horse La. ST1 27 B5
ckwells Row. ST6 27 B3
eak Pl. ST6 27 A1
tteslow St. ST1 27 D6
ulton St. ST1 27 D3
undary St. ST1 27 B4
w St. ST1 27 C4
wlers Clo. ST1 27 A3
wness St. ST1 27 B3
ewery St. ST1 27 C4
anson Av. ST6 27 C1
oad St. ST1 27 B6
ockley Sq. ST1 27 C5
omley St. ST1 27 A4
omley St. ST1 27 A4
oom St. ST1 27 C4
oomfield Pl Nth. ST1 27 A6
oomfield Pl Sth. ST1 27 A6
unswick St. ST1 27 C5
cknall New Rd. ST1 27 D5
cknall Old Rd. ST1 27 D5
rnley St. ST1 27 D3
rton Pl. ST1 27 C5
xton St. ST1 27 D1
ldbeck Pl. ST1 27 D5
nnon St. ST1 27 B6
pe St. ST1 27 C4
sewell Rd. ST6 27 C1
vendish St. ST1 27 A6
cil Av. ST1 27 B4
ntury St. ST1 27 A4
arles St. ST1 27 C6
eapside. ST1 27 C6
ell St. ST1 27 D3
elwood St. ST1 27 B4
ichester Walk. ST1 27 D4
orlton Rd. ST1 27 D2
urch Ter. ST1 27 A3
ough St. ST1 27 A6
bridge Rd. ST1 27 A5
mmercial Rd. ST1 27 D6
urtway Dri. ST1 27 D1
ane St. ST1 27 B3
ep La. ST6 27 B2
omwell St. ST1 27 D2
ossway Rd. ST6 27 C1
own St. ST1 27 B6
rystal St. ST6 27 B2
ryfields Way. ST1 27 C1
ne Walk. ST1 27 D5
vison St. ST6 27 A1
nbigh St. ST1 27 A4
rby St. ST1 27 D6
rwent St. ST1 27 A3
kenson Rd East. ST6
kinson Rd West. ST6
ke St. ST1 27 C1
bson St. ST6 27 D4
uglas St. ST1 27 B1
ver St. ST1 27 B3
esden St. ST1 27 D4
kes St. ST1 27 D4
stbank Rd. ST1 27 D5
stwood Rd. ST1 27 A4
ton St. ST1 27 D6
gware St. ST1 27 D5
ler Pl. ST6 27 A3
er Rd. ST6 27 A2
ler St. ST6 27 A3
n St. ST6 27 D3
s St. ST6 27 B1
ery St. ST6 27 A2
uria Rd. ST1 27 A2
uria Vale Rd. ST1 27 A5
mouth Gro. ST6 27 A6
rfax St. ST1 27 A1
sting St. ST1 27 D3
ntsham Gro. ST1 27 D4
ser St. ST6 27 C4
ee Trade St. ST1 27 B1
rnival St. ST6 27 D4
rnet St. ST1 27 B2
rth St. ST1 27 A6
bbins St. ST1 27 D5
lchrist Ct, 27 D3
Emery St. ST6 27 A2
man Pl. ST1 27 C5
ana St. ST1 27 D6
ass St. ST1 27 C5
over St. ST1 27 C5
odson St. ST1 27 C5
rdon Av. ST1 27 C1

Grafton St. ST1 27 D4
Grange St. ST6 27 A2
Granville Av. ST1 27 D2
Greville St. ST1 27 B5
Greyhound Way. ST1 27 A3
Grove St. ST6 27 A2
Hanley Rd. ST1 27 D1
Hanover St. ST1 27 B4
Harley St. ST1 27 D6
Hassal St. ST1 27 D6
Hawthorn St. ST6 27 A2
Hazelwood Clo. ST6 27 C2
Hillary St. ST6 27 B2
Hillchurch St. ST1 27 C5
Hillcrest St. ST1 27 D5
Hobart St. ST6 27 A1
Hodnet Gro. ST1 27 B3
Holder St. ST1 27 B3
Hope St. ST1 27 B4
Hordley St. ST1 27 D5
Hot La. ST6 27 A1
Howson St. ST1 27 D6
Hughes St. ST6 27 A1
Hulton St. ST1 27 D4
Huntbach St. ST1 27 C5
INDUSTRIAL & RETAIL:
Britannia Park
Ind Est. ST6 27 B1
Far Green Ind Est.
ST1 27 D3
New Forest Ind Est.
ST1 27 C4
The Octagon
Shopping Pk. ST1 27 A5
Jasper St. ST1 27 C6
Jervis St. ST1 27 D4
John Bright St. ST1 27 D4
John St. ST1 27 C6
Josiah Wedgwood St.
ST1 27 A6
Keelings Rd. ST1 27 D4
Kelvin Av. ST1 27 D2
Kibworth Gro. ST1 27 C3
King George St. ST1 27 D4
Kingswinford Pl. ST6 27 D1
Kirby St. ST6 27 A2
Lamb St. ST1 27 C5
Langdale Cres. ST1 27 D1
Leek New Rd. ST1 27 A2
Lichfield St. ST1 27 C6
Lincoln St. ST1 27 D6
Lindley St. ST6 27 B1
Linfield St. ST1 27 B5
Linoop St. ST1 27 D5
Lockett St. ST1 27 D3
Loftus St. ST1 27 B4
Louvain Av. ST1 27 D1
Lower Bryan St. ST1 27 C3
Lower Foundry St. ST1 27 C5
Lower Mayer St. ST1 27 D4
Lowther St. ST1 27 A4
Ludlow St. ST1 27 D5
Malam St. ST1 27 B4
Market Sq. ST1 27 C5
Marsden St. ST1 27 D5
Marsh St Nth. ST1 27 B5
Marsh St Sth. ST1 27 B5
Martin St. ST6 27 B1
Mawdesley St. ST1 27 A2
Mayer St. ST1 27 C4
Maylea Cres. ST6 27 C1
Meigh St. ST1 27 C5
Melrose Av. ST1 27 D1
Merrick St. ST1 27 D3
Mersey St. ST1 27 B6
Milburn Rd. ST6 27 B2
Milgreen Av. ST1 27 D1
Miller St. ST1 27 D1
Moorcroft Rd. ST6 27 B1
Moore St. ST6 27 A1
Morley St. ST1 27 B6
Moston St. ST1 27 D3
Mount Pleasant. ST1 27 A6
Mount St. ST1 27 D4
Moxley Av. ST1 27 D1
Mulberry St. ST1 27 D6
Mulgrave St. ST1 27 B1
Myatt St. ST1 27 D4
Mynors St. ST1 27 D4
Nelson Pl. ST1 27 D6
New Hall St. ST1 27 B5
Nile St. ST6 27 A1
North Rd. ST6 27 A1
Northam Rd. ST1 27 D2
Old Hall St. ST1 27 C5
Old Town Rd. ST1 27 C4
Orb St. ST1 27 C5
Orgreave St. ST6 27 A1
Oxford Av. ST1 27 D3
Pall Mall. ST1 27 C6
Parker St. ST1 27 B5

Parliament Row. ST1 27 C5
Parliament Sq. ST1 27 C5
Pavillion Dri. ST1 27 A4
Penarth Gro. ST1 27 B4
Percy St. ST1 27 C5
Perry Clo. ST1 27 D6
Piccadilly. ST1 27 C6
Picton St. ST1 27 D4
Plough St. ST1 27 D4
Podmore St. ST6 27 A1
Portland St. ST1 27 B4
Potteries Way. ST1 27 B4
Powell St. ST1 27 A4
Providence St. ST1 27 D3
Purbeck St. ST1 27 B2
Quadrant Rd. ST1 27 C5
Ranelagh St. ST1 27 B3
Ratton St. ST1 27 D5
Raymond Av. ST1 27 B4
Redman Gro. ST6 27 C1
Remer St. ST6 27 A3
Rhodes St. ST1 27 D3
Rhondda Av. ST6 27 C1
Ringland Clo. ST1 27 D5
Rixdale Clo. ST1 27 C4
Robson St. ST1 27 B6
Rosevean Clo. ST1 27 B4
Rushton Gro. ST6 27 A2
Rushton Rd. ST6 27 A2
Rutland St. ST1 27 A4
St Andrews Cres. ST1 27 D2
St Ann St. ST1 27 D5
*St Ann Walk,
St Ann St. ST1 27 D5
St James St. ST1 27 B6
St John St. ST1 27 D4
St Luke St. ST1 27 D6
St Peters Walk. ST6 27 A2
Salcombe Pl. ST1 27 D1
Sampson St. ST1 27 B4
Sandbach Rd. ST6 27 B2
Sandon St. ST1 27 A6
Sceptre St. ST1 27 B6
Sefton St. ST1 27 A6
Severn St. ST1 27 A3
Shaw St. ST1 27 A4
Sheldon St. ST6 27 A1
Sidcot Pl. ST1 27 D1
Slippery La. ST1 27 B6
Sneyd St. ST6 27 B2
Southampton St. ST1 27 C4
Spa St. ST6 27 A1
Stadium Ct. ST1 27 A3
Stafford La. ST1 27 C5
Stafford St. ST1 27 C5
Stansgate Pl. ST1 27 B4
Stanway Av. ST6 27 C1
Statham St. ST1 27 B6
Stedman St. ST1 27 D3
Stokesay Gro. ST6 27 A1
Stonor St. ST6 27 A2
Stubbs La. ST1 27 D6
Sudlow St. ST6 27 B1
Tewson Grn. ST6 27 C1
The Coppice. ST6 27 C1
Tierney St. ST1 27 C5
Tontine St. ST1 27 C5
Tor Rd. ST1 27 B1
Town Rd. ST1 27 C4
Trafalgar St. ST1 27 C4
Trinity St. ST1 27 B5
Turner St. ST1 27 D4
Twemlow St. ST1 27 A6
Union St. ST1 27 C4
Unity Av. ST1 27 D1
Upper Hillchurch St.
ST1 27 D4
Upper Huntbach St.
ST1 27 D5
Walley Pl. ST6 27 A1
Walley St. ST6 27 A1
Walney Gro. ST1 27 C3
Warburton St. ST1 27 A1
Warner St. ST1 27 B6
Waterloo Rd. ST1 27 A1
Waterloo St. ST1 27 D6
Wayte St. ST1 27 B3
Weaver St. ST1 27 A1
Well St. ST1 27 D5
Wellington Ct. ST1 27 D5
Wellington Rd. ST1 27 D5
Wellington St. ST1 27 D6
Wellington Ter. ST1 27 D5
Wensleydale Clo. ST1 27 C1
Westwood Ct. ST1 27 B4
Whitehaven Dri. ST1 27 B4
Windermere St. ST1 27 B4
Windmill St. ST1 27 D5
Winifred St. ST1 27 B4
Woodall St. ST1 27 B3
Woodward St. ST1 27 D2

York St. ST1 27 B4

HEATH HAYES

Acorn Clo. WS11 39 B5
Adelaide Dri. WS11 39 D4
Almond Clo. WS11 39 B5
Alnwick Clo. WS12 39 C5
Alston Clo. WS12 39 D5
Amber Gro. WS11 39 B4
Ansty Dri. WS12 39 C5
Apple Walk. WS11 39 A5
Appledore Clo. WS12 39 D4
Asquith Dri. WS11 39 B5
Atlee Gro. WS11 39 B5
Attingham Dri. WS11 39 A5
Avenue Rd. WS12 39 C5
Badgers Way. WS12 39 B5
Baldwin Gro. WS11 39 B5
Bank St. WS12 39 D6
Barber Clo. WS12 39 C4
Beacon Way. WS12 39 D4
Birchfields Clo. WS12 39 C6
Blithfield Pl. WS11 39 A5
Boston Clo. WS12 39 D5
Bourne Clo. WS11 39 C5
Brampton Rd. WS12 39 D5
Brisbane Way. WS12 39 D4
Bristol Clo. WS11 39 A6
Bronte. WS11 39 B5
Brooklyn Rd. WS12 39 C6
Buckingham Pl. WS12 39 B6
Burdock Clo. WS11 39 A4
Callaghan Gro. WS11 39 B5
Cannock Rd. WS12 39 B6
Canterbury Way. WS12 39 C5
Carlton Clo. WS12 39 C5
Chapel St. WS12 39 D6
Chaplain Rd. WS12 39 C5
Charlock Gro. WS11 39 B4
Charterfield Dri. WS12 39 C6
Chester Clo. WS11 39 A6
Chestnut Clo. WS11 39 B5
Chichester Dri. WS12 39 A6
Claygate Rd. WS12 39 D4
Cleeton St. WS12 39 C6
Clover Meadows.
WS12 39 B6
Condor Gro. WS12 39 B6
Cromwell Rd. WS12 39 C6
Cross St. WS12 39 D5
Cuckoo Clo. WS11 39 A4
Darwin Clo. WS11 39 D5
Deavall Way. WS11 39 A4
Denbury Clo. WS11 39 C5
Diamond Gro. WS11 39 B4
Dorset Rd. WS12 39 D6
Dugdale Clo. WS11 39 B6
Eagle Gro. WS12 39 B6
Eden Clo. WS12 39 D5
Edgemoor Mdw. WS12 39 B6
Edmonton Clo. WS11 39 A5
Elder Clo. WS11 39 B5
Ely Clo. WS11 39 A6
Fairfield Clo. WS12 39 C5
Firecrest Clo. WS11 39 B5
Foxhill Clo. WS12 39 C5
Fremantle Dri. WS12 39 D4
Gladstone Rd. WS12 39 C6
Gladstone Rd. WS12 39 C6
Gloucester Way. WS12 39 A6
Gorsemoor Rd. WS12 39 B6
Goya Clo. WS11 39 B4
Green Mdws. WS12 39 B6
Greig Ct. WS11 39 B5
Handel Ct. WS11 39 A5
Harebell Clo. WS11 39 C5
Hartlebury Clo. WS11 39 B4
Hawks Grn La. WS11 39 A6
Hayes Way. WS12 39 A6
Heath Way. WS11 39 A5
Heathland Clo. WS12 39 C5
Hemlock Way. WS11 39 A5
Hickery Ct. WS11 39 A5
Highfield Rd. WS12 39 C5
Hill St. WS12 39 B4
Hobart Rd. WS12 39 D5
Hodnet Pl. WS11 39 A5
Holt Cres. WS11 39 A5
Hopton Mdws. WS12 39 B6
Houston Clo. WS11 39 B6
Hudson Clo. WS11 39 A5
Huron Clo. WS11 39 B5
Hyssop Clo. WS11 39 A4
INDUSTRIAL & RETAIL:
Chasewood Ind Est.
WS12 39 D6

Ingestre Clo. WS11 39 A6
Jade Gro. WS11 39 B5
Kensington Pl. WS12 39 B6
Kent Pl. WS12 39 D6
Kestrel Gro. WS12 39 B6
Kielder Clo. WS12 39 D5
Knighton Rd. WS12 39 D4
Langholm Dri. WS12 39 C5
Langtree Clo. WS12 39 C6
Lichfield Rd. WS11 39 A6
Lloyd George Gro.
WS11 39 B5
Ludlow Clo. WS11 39 B4
Lyndhurst Rd. WS12 39 C6
Marigold Clo. WS11 39 B4
Meadow Way. WS12 39 B6
Melbourne Rd. WS12 39 D5
Michigan Clo. WS11 39 A5
Mill Cres. WS11 39 A5
Millers Vale. WS12 39 C6
Mozart Ct. WS11 39 B5
Newlands Ct. WS12 39 C6
Newlands La. WS12 39 C6
Nicholls Way. WS12 39 C6
Osprey Gro. WS11 39 B5
Otterburn Clo. WS12 39 D5
Peterborough Dri.
WS12 39 B6
Picasso Clo. WS11 39 B4
Primrose Mdw. WS11 39 B4
Redbrook Clo. WS12 39 C5
Rembrandt Clo. WS11 39 B5
Rochester Way. WS12 39 B6
Rosebay Mdw. WS11 39 B6
Rothbury Grn. WS12 39 D6
Rutland Rd. WS12 39 D6
St Johns Ct. WS12 39 D5
St Lawrence Dri. WS11 39 A5
St Pauls Clo. WS11 39 A6
Salisbury Dri. WS12 39 A6
Sam Barber Ct. WS12 39 D5
Sapphire Dri. WS11 39 B4
Shirehall Pl. WS11 39 A5
Shugboro Way. WS11 39 A6
Sidon Hill Way. WS11 39 A4
Spindleywood Clo.
WS12 39 B6
Spode Clo. WS11 39 B5
Squirrel Clo. WS11 39 B5
Stafford St. WS12 39 D6
The Coppice. WS12 39 D6
Thistledown Dri. WS12 39 B6
Trentham Clo. WS11 39 A5
Truro Pl. WS12 39 B6
Turner Clo. WS11 39 B4
Turquoise Gro. WS11 39 B4
Tutbury Clo. WS11 39 A4
Van Gogh Clo. WS11 39 B5
Weston Clo. WS11 39 A6
Wheatlands Clo. WS11 39 B5
Willowherb Clo. WS11 39 B5
Wilson Gro. WS11 39 B5
Wimblebury Rd. WS12 39 D6
Woodford Way. WS12 39 B5
Woodpecker Way.
WS11 39 A4

HUNTINGTON/ HEDNESFORD

Abbey St. WS12 29 E2
Abbots Field. WS11 28 C3
Addison Clo. WS11 28 C4
Albert St. WS11 28 C5
Albert St. WS12 29 G4
Albion Pl. WS11 28 C5
Almond Rd. WS11 28 B1
Alpine Dri. WS12 29 G5
Amber Gro. WS12 29 G6
Andover Pl. WS11 29 E5
Anglesey Cres. WS12 29 F4
Anglesey St. WS12 29 F4
Anglia Rd. WS11 28 B6
Anne Cres. WS11 28 C3
Apollo Clo. WS11 29 E3
Ardgay Av. WS12 28 D2
Arnotdale Dri. WS12 28 D2
Arran Clo. WS12 29 E6
Arthur St. WS11 28 D5
Ash Gro. WS11 28 D5
Ash Vw. WS12 29 E2
Ashbourne Clo. WS11 29 E5
Ashdale Clo. WS12 28 A2
Badger Clo. WS12 28 B2+
Bailey Clo. WS11 29 E5
Bakers Way. WS12 29 F3
Balmoral Rd. WS11 28 D2
Baltic Clo. WS11 28 C5
Barley Clo. WS12 29 F3

Barnard Way. WS11 28 D6
Bath Rd. WS11 28 C3
Bedford Pl. WS12 29 F4
Beech Ct.WS12 29 F1
Beech Gro. WS12 28 B1
Beech Pine Clo. WS12 29 E1
Bell Dri. WS12 29 G1
Belt Rd. WS12 28 C3
Benion Rd. WS11 28 D4
Berry Hill. WS12 29 F5
Bevan Lee Rd. WS11 28 B5
Beverley Hill. WS12 29 G2
Bilberry Bank. WS11 28 C3
Bilberry Clo. WS12 28 A3
Blake Clo. WS11 29 E4
Blewitt St. WS12 29 E2
Bluebell Clo. WS12 29 F3
Bondway. WS12 28 D1
Booth St. WS12 29 F3
Boswell Rd. WS11 28 B5
Bowes Dri. WS11 28 D5
Bracken Clo. WS12 29 G1
Bracken Rd. WS12 28 A3
Bradbury La. WS12 29 E1
Bradford St. WS11 29 E4
Braemar Gdns. WS12 28 D2
Bramble Dri. WS12 29 G1
Brindley Cres. WS12 29 G1
Brindley Heath Rd. WS12 29 G2
Broadway. WS12 28 D2
Bromley Clo. WS12 29 F2
Brooke Rd. WS12 28 D2
Brookland Rd. WS11 29 E5
Broomhill Bank. WS11 28 C5
Broomhill Clo. WS11 28 C5
Brunswick Rd. WS11 28 C6
Buckthorn Clo. WS12 28 D1
Bunyan Pl. WS11 28 C5
Burdock Clo. WS12 29 F6
Burgoyne St. WS11 29 E4
Burleigh Clo. WS12 29 E1
Burns St. WS11 28 D5
Buttermere Clo. WS11 29 E6
Byron Pl. WS11 28 C4
Cambria St. WS11 28 B5
Camelot Clo. WS11 28 D5
Cannock Rd. WS11 28 D6
Cardigan Pl. WS12 29 G4
Cardinal Way. WS12 28 B6
Carmel Clo. WS12 29 G4
Cavans St. WS11 28 C4
Cecil St. WS11 28 D5
Cedar Hill. WS11 28 D6
Celtic Rd. WS11 28 C6
Cemetery Rd. WS11 28 B5
Central Av. WS11 28 D4
Chacery Dri. WS12 29 F1
Chaffinch Clo. WS12 29 E5
Chalicot Dri. WS12 28 D2
Charlemont Clo. WS12 29 G5
Charlock Gro. WS12 29 G6
Charnwood Clo. WS12 29 G5
Chase Wk. WS12 28 A4
Chaseley Av. WS11 28 A6
Chaseside Dri. WS11 29 E6
Chatsworth Dri. WS11 29 E5
Cherry Bank. WS12 29 F3
Cherry Tree Rd. WS12 28 B1
Chetwynd Gdns. WS11 28 B6
Cheviot Rise. WS12 29 F4
Church Hill. WS12 29 G4
Church St. WS11 29 E5
Clarion Way. WS11 28 C4
Cleveland Dri. WS11 29 E5
Cobden Clo. WS12 29 G2
Cock Sparrow La. WS12 28 A2
Columbian Dri. WS11 28 D6
Columbian Way. WS11 28 D6
Common La. WS11 29 E6
Common Vw. WS12 29 F1
Common Walk. WS12 28 A4
Conifer Clo. WS12 29 E1
Copperkins Rd. WS12 29 H6
Coppermill Clo. WS12 28 D2
Cornhill. WS11 28 C4
Cornwall Rd. WS12 29 F4
Corsican Dri. WS12 28 D1
Cottage Clo. WS12 29 G4
Crab La. WS11 29 E6
Croxley Clo. WS12 29 G5
Cuckoo Clo. WS12 29 F6
Cumberland Rd. WS11 29 E5
Curlew Hill. WS11 29 E5
Cygnet Clo. WS12 29 G2
Daisy Bank. WS12 28 D1
Deavall Way. WS11 29 F6
Deer Clo. WS12 28 B2
Denmark Rise. WS12 29 H2
Diamond Gro. WS12 29 G6
Dovedale. WS11 29 E4
Downes Way. WS11 28 A6
Dual Way. WS12 28 A1
*Durberville Walk, Melbury Way. WS11 28 D6
East Cannock Rd. WS11 29 E6
Eastern Way. WS11 29 E6
Ebenezer St. WS12 29 E2
Edison Clo. WS12 29 G1
Edward St. WS11 28 C4
Elgar Clo. WS11 28 C4
Elizabeth Rd. WS11 28 C3
Elm Gro. WS12 28 B1
Elmwood Clo. WS11 29 E6
Eskrett St. WS12 29 F4
Essex Dri. WS12 29 F4
Exonbury Wk. WS11 28 D6
Fallow Field Rd. WS11 28 C6
Farm Clo. WS12 29 G6
Fawn Clo. WS12 28 A3
Fern Rd. WS11 28 B4
*Festival Ct, Clarion Way. WS11 28 C3
Festival Mews. WS12 28 D3
Field St. WS11 28 D6
Fieldhouse Rd. WS12 28 D2
Fir Clo. WS12 28 B1
Fircroft Clo. WS11 29 E6
Florence St. WS12 29 E2
Forge St. WS12 29 G5
Foster Av. WS11 28 D3
Foxes Rake. WS11 28 C6
Foxfields Way. WS12 28 B2
Foxglove Wk. WS12 29 G1
Foxglove Way. WS12 29 H5
Gaelic Rd. WS11 28 B5
Garrick Rd. WS11 28 B5
George St. WS12 29 G4
Glen Clo. WS11 28 C4
Glencoe Dri. WS11 29 E5
Glendale Gdns. WS11 28 D4
Glendawn Clo. WS11 29 E5
Glendene Rd. WS12 29 G2
Gorse Dri. WS12 28 B4
Gorse Way. WS12 29 G1
Grace Moore Ct. WS11 28 D4
Granary Clo. WS12 29 E3
Grasmere Pl. WS11 28 C4
Gravel La. WS12 28 A3
Gray Rd. WS11 28 D3
Green Slade Gro. WS12 29 G2
Green Heath Rd. WS12 29 E1
Greenwood Pk. WS12 29 F1
Gresham Rd. WS11 28 D6
Grimley Way. WS11 28 D4
Haig Clo. WS11 29 E4
Hamelin St. WS11 28 C6
Hardie Grn. WS11 28 D6
Hartlebury Clo. WS12 29 F6
Hawks Green La. WS11 29 E6
Hawkyard Clo. WS11 29 E5
Hawthorne Rd. WS12 28 B1
Heath Gap Rd. WS11 28 D6
Heath St. WS12 29 E1
Heathbank Dri. WS12 28 A3
Heather Dri. WS12 28 B4
Heather Valley. WS12 29 G3
Hedgerow Clo. WS12 28 D1
Hemlock Way. WS12 29 F6
Hereford Rd. WS12 29 F4
Herondale. WS12 29 F5
Hewston Croft. WS12 29 H5
High Grange. WS11 29 E4
High Mount St. WS12 29 F3
Highfield Ct. WS11 29 E4
Highland Rd. WS12 28 A5
Hill St. WS12 29 G5
Hillside Clo. WS12 29 E1
Hodson Way. WS11 29 F6
Holly La. WS12 28 A2
Holly St. WS11 28 C3
Howard Cres. WS12 29 F2
Huntington Terrace Rd. WS11 28 D5
Huntsmans Rise. WS12 28 A1
Hyssop Clo. WS12 29 F6
INDUSTRIAL & RETAIL:
Advance Business Pk. WS11 29 F6
Ash Park Ind Est. WS11 29 E6
Beechwood Business Pk. WS11 29 F6
*Brindleys Business Pk. East Cannok Rd. WS11 29 E6
Cannoock Motor Village. WS11 29 F6
Greens Ind Est. WS12 29 G2
Hawkes Grn Ind Est. WS12 29 E6
Image Business Pk. WS11 29 F6
Keys Business Pk. WS12 29 H5
Littleton Business Pk. WS12 28 A2
Oaklands Business Pk. WS12 29 F5
Ridings Pk. WS11 29 E6
James St. WS11 28 D4
John St. WS11 28 D4
Johnson Rd. WS11 28 B5
Keats Av. WS11 28 C4
Kelvin Dri. WS11 29 E6
Kenilworth Dri. WS11 28 B5
Kenmore Av. WS11 28 D2
Keys Clo. WS12 29 G6
Keys Park Rd. WS12 29 G6
Kingfisher Dri. WS12 29 F4
Kings Av. WS12 29 G5
Kingsley Av. WS12 29 G2
Kingsway. WS11 29 E4
Kinross Av. WS12 28 D2
Lansbury Dri. WS11 28 C5
Larchwood Dri. WS12 29 E5
Laurel Dri. WS12 29 H5
Leaf Down Ct. WS12 29 G5
Lee Wk. WS11 29 E4
Levetts Hollow. WS12 29 G6
Lichen Clo. WS12 28 A3
Lime Rd. WS12 28 B1
Limepit La. WS12 28 A2
Linden Vw. WS12 29 F5
Ling Rd. WS12 28 A4
Linnet Clo. WS12 28 B2
Linwood Dri. WS12 28 D2
Littleton Dri. WS12 28 A2
Littleworth Hill. WS12 29 H5
Littleworth Rd. WS12 29 G5
Lomax Rd. WS12 29 E1
Long Croft. WS12 28 A5
Longfellow Pl. WS11 28 C5
Lotus Dri. WS11 28 C3
Lovatt Pl. WS11 28 C4
Lower Rd. WS12 29 F5
Lowland Rd. WS12 28 A4
Lysander Way. WS11 28 C6
McGeough Wk. WS11 29 E4
McGhie St. WS12 29 F3
Maple Dri. WS12 29 G2
Marcon Pl. WS12 29 G1
Margaret Dri. WS11 28 C3
Marigold Clo. WS12 29 G6
Marina Cres. WS12 29 E3
Market St. WS12 29 F3
Marston Rd. WS12 28 D3
Mary St. WS12 29 F2
Masefield Gro. WS11 28 C5
Matlock Dri. WS11 29 E5
Mavis Rd. WS12 29 F2
Maycroft. WS12 28 D1
Meadow Croft. WS12 28 A5
Meadow Hill Dri. WS11 28 D6
Meadowlark Clo. WS12 29 F5
Meadway Clo. WS12 29 G6
Melbury Way. WS11 28 D6
Melrose Dri. WS12 28 D2
Mercury Rd. WS11 29 E4
Metcalfe Clo. WS12 29 F2
Midhurst Dri. WS12 29 G1
Midland Rd. WS12 28 A4
Millicent Clo. WS12 29 F2
Millpool Rd. WS12 29 F2
Milton Rd. WS11 28 C5
Mitcham Clo. WS12 28 D2
Montrose Clo. WS11 28 D3
Moore St. WS12 29 G2
Moorland Rd. WS11 28 C4
Moreton St. WS11 28 D4
Moss Cres. WS12 28 B4
Moss Rd. WS11 29 E6
Moss St. WS11 29 E5
Mount Av. WS12 29 F2
Mount Side St. WS12 29 F2
Mount St. WS12 29 F1
Mountain Pine. WS12 29 E1
Mulberry Rd. WS11 28 C6
Muldoon Clo. WS11 29 E4
Naden Ho. WS12 28 A4
New Link Rd. WS12 29 H6
New St. WS12 29 G4
Newhall Cres. WS11 29 F6
Newhall Gdns. WS11 28 D6
Nightingale Clo. WS12 28 A2
Oak Av. WS12 28 B1
Oakhill Rd. WS11 28 D6
Odin Clo. WS11 28 D3
Old Fallow Rd. WS11 28 C6
Old Hednesford Rd. WS11 29 E6
Orion Way. WS11 28 D4
Partridge Clo. WS12 28 B1
Passfield Av. WS12 29 F2
Pasture Gate. WS11 28 A6
Pattedale Rd. WS11 29 E5
Pavilion View. WS12 29 G2
Pear Tree Clo. WS12 28 A1
Pendle Hill. WS12 29 F4
Petersfield. WS11 28 D5
Phillip Gro. WS11 28 C3
Phoenix Rd. WS11 29 E6
Pillaton Dri. WS12 28 A3
Pinewood Av. WS11 28 B5
Platt St. WS11 29 E4
Pope Gro. WS12 28 D2
Poplar Av. WS11 28 D5
Prince St. WS11 28 C3
Princess St. WS11 28 C4
Priory Rd. WS12 29 H5
Prospect Manor Grange. WS12 29 F6
Pye Green Rd. WS11 28 C6
Queen St. WS11 29 E4
Radnor Rise. WS12 29 F4
Raven Clo, Huntington. WS12 28 B2
Raven Clo, Littleworth. WS12 29 H5
Rawnsley Rd. WS12 29 G2
Redhill Rd. WS11 28 C5
Redwing Dri. WS12 28 B2
Redwood Dri. WS11 28 D6
Reservoir Rd. WS12 29 H5
Richmond Clo. WS11 29 E4
Rigby Dri. WS11 28 C5
Robin Clo. WS12 28 A2
Rose Hill. WS12 28 D1
Rowan Rd. WS11 28 A6
Rowley Clo. WS12 29 E1
Rugeley Rd. WS12 29 G2
Rydall Clo. WS12 29 E1
St Aidans Rd. WS11 28 C4
St Chads Clo. WS11 29 E5
St Peters Rd. WS12 29 G4
*St Stephens Ct, Kings Av. WS12 29 G5
Sandpiper Clo. WS12 29 G2
Sankey Rd. WS11 28 D5
Sapphire Dri. WS12 29 G6
Saturn Rd. WS11 28 D3
Scotia Rd. WS11 28 B6
Shaftsbury Way. WS12 29 F2
Shakespeare Gro. WS11 28 B5
Sharon Way. WS12 29 G5
Shelly Rd. WS11 28 C4
Sheraton Clo. WS12 28 D2
Sherbourne Av. WS12 29 H5
Sherwood Dri. WS11 29 E5
Short St. WS11 28 D6
Sidon Hill Way. WS12 29 F6
Silver Birch Rd. WS12 28 B1
Silver Fir Clo. WS12 29 E1
Simcox St. WS12 29 H4
Skylark Clo. WS12 28 B2
Smalley Clo. WS11 29 E4
Smillie Pl. WS11 28 D5
Snowdon Rd. WS11 28 C3
Somerset Pl. WS11 28 C5
Southbourne Pl. WS11 28 B6
Speedy Clo. WS11 28 C4
Splash La. WS12 29 G5
Springfield Rise. WS12 29 F2
Squirrel Clo. WS12 28 B2
Stafford La. WS12 29 F4
Stafford Rd. WS12 28 A2
Stag Dri. WS12 28 A2
Stagborough Dri. WS12 29 F4
Stanley Rd. WS11 29 E3
Station Rd. WS12 29 F3
Stevens Dri. WS12 29 G2
Stone Pine Clo. WS12 28 D1
Stratford Way. WS11 28 D4
Stringers Hill. WS12 29 G2
Sunley Dri. WS12 29 G2
Sunrise Hill. WS12 29 F3
Sussex Dri. WS12 29 F4
Swallow Clo. WS12 28 B2
Swallowfields Dri. WS11 29 E5
Sycamore Grn. WS11 28 C3
Sycamore Way. WS12 28 B1
Taplow Pl. WS11 28 D5
Teddesley Ct. WS11 28 B5
Teddesley Way. WS12 28 A3
Telford Gro. WS12 29 E2
The Poplars. WS11 28 C5
The Sidings. WS12 29 G2
Thor Clo. WS11 29 E4
Thornhill Rd. WS12 28 D2
Tranter Cres. WS11 29 F6
Trent Rd. WS11 28 C3
Turquoise Gro. WS12 29 G6
Tutbury Clo. WS12 29 F6
Ulster Clo. WS11 29
*Uxbridge Ct, Uxbridge St. WS12 29
Uxbridge St. WS12 29
Valley Rd. WS12 29
Vermont Grn. WS11 28
Victoria St, Broomhill. WS11 28
Victoria St, Hednesford. WS12 29
View St. WS11 28
Viewfield Av. WS12 28
Walkers Rise. WS12 29
Walnut Clo. WS11 28
Walnut Dri. WS11 28
Ward St. WS11 28
Wardle Pl. WS11 28
Wells Clo. WS11 28
Wesley Pl. WS12 29
West Hill Av. WS12 29
Westbourne Av. WS11 28
Western Rd. WS12 29
Westminster Rd. WS11 28
White Bark Clo. WS12 28
Whitethorn Clo. WS12 29
Whitfield Av. WS12 29
Wilcox Av. WS12 29
William Morris Gro. WS11 28
Willow Walk. WS12 28
Winchester Rd. WS11 29
Windrush Rd. WS11 28
Winsor Av. WS12 29
Wood La. WS12 29
Woodford End. WS11 28
Woodland Clo. WS12 29
Woodland Ct. WS12 28
Woodpecker Way. WS12 29
Woodside Pl. WS11 28
Woodstock Dri. WS12 28
Wootton Clo. WS11 29
Wordsworth Clo. WS11 28
Wrekin Vw. WS12 28
Wrights Av. WS11 28
Wyvern Gro. WS12 29

KIDSGROVE

Acacia Gdns. ST7 31
Acres Nook Rd. ST6 30
Albany St. ST6 31
Alder Clo. ST7 31
Alice St. ST6 31
Ancaster St. ST6 31
Andrew St. ST6 31
Anne Ct. ST7 30
Anne St. ST6 31
Ash View. ST6 31
Ashenough Rd. ST7 30
Astbury Clo. ST7 31
Attwood St. ST7 31
Aubrey St. ST6 31
Audley Rd. ST7 30
Avon Clo. ST7 31
Back Heathcote St. ST7 30
Banbury St. ST7 30
Barrie Gdns. ST7 30
Bedford Rd. ST7 30
Beech Dri. ST7 30
Beeston Vw. ST7 31
Bevan Av. ST7 30
Birchall Av. ST6 31
Birches Way. ST7 31
Birkdale Dri. ST7 31
Bishops Clo. ST7 30
Boat Horse Rd, Kidsgrove. ST7 30
Boat Horse Rd, Ravenscliffe. ST6 31
Bosley Gro. ST6 31
Bourne Rd. ST7 30
Brakespeare St. ST6 31
Briarswood. ST7 31
Brieryhurst Rd. ST7 31
Brights Av. ST7 31
Brindley Clo. ST7 30
Broadfield Rd. ST6 31
Browning Gro. ST7 30
Bullocks Ho Rd. ST7 31
Burnaby Rd. ST6 31
Burnfield Gro. ST6 31
Burns Clo. ST7 30
Butt La. ST7 30
Byron Ct. ST7 30
Capper Clo. ST7 31
Cartlich St. ST6 31
Castle View Rd. ST7 31

LEEK

Pickford Rd. ST13 33 E4
Pickwood Av. ST13 33 F4
Picton St. ST13 32 D3
Pitcher La. ST13 33 G4
Portland St. ST13 33 F3
Portland St,
 North. ST13 33 F3
Portland St,
 South. ST13 33 F4
Prince Charles Av.
 ST13 33 G2
Prince St. ST13 33 F2
Princess Av. ST13 33 G1
Priory Av. ST13 33 G1
Prospect Rd. ST13 33 G4
Provost Pl. ST13 33 F2
Pump St. ST13 33 F2
Queen St. ST13 33 G1
Queens Dri. ST13 33 G1
Regent St. ST13 33 E3
Roche Av. ST13 33 G1
Rochford Clo. ST13 32 B4
Rose Bank St. ST13 33 E3
Rownall Vw. ST13 32 C5
Russel St. ST13 33 E4
St Edward St. ST13 33 E4
Salisbury St. ST13 32 D3
Sandon St. ST13 33 E5
Sandybrook Clo. ST13 33 F6
School Clo. ST13 32 C5
*School St,
 West St. ST13 32 D3
Selborne St. ST13 32 D5
Selborne St. ST13 33 E5
Sharron Dri. ST13 33 G4
Shaw Pl. ST13 33 F3
Sheep St. ST13 33 E4
Shipburn Rd. ST13 33 F3
Shirley St. ST13 32 D4
Shoobridge St. ST13 33 E4
Silk St. ST13 33 E3
Sneyd Av. ST13 32 D4
Sneyd St. ST13 32 D4
Southbank St. ST13 33 E4
Southlands Clo. ST13 32 C3
Spencer Av. ST13 33 E4
Spring Gdns. ST13 32 C4
Springfield Clo. ST13 33 F4
Springfield Ct. ST13 33 F3
Springfield Rd. ST13 33 F4
Stanley St. ST13 33 E4
Station St. ST13 32 D4
*Steep Row,
 Compton. ST13 33 E4
Stockwell St. ST13 33 E3
Strangman St. ST13 32 D4
Sunnyhill Rd. ST13 32 C6
Swallow Croft. ST13 32 C6
Talbot St. ST13 33 E4
Tatton Clo. ST13 32 B5
The Crescent. ST13 33 F3
The Sleeve. ST13 32 C5
The Walks. ST13 32 D4
The Willows. ST13 32 C4
Thomas St. ST13 32 C3
Thorncliffe Rd. ST13 33 H2
Thorncliffe Vw. ST13 33 G1
Thornfield Av. ST13 33 G4
Thornhill Rd. ST13 32 C5
Tittesworth Av. ST13 33 F2
Trafford La. ST13 33 G4
Union St. ST13 33 E4
Valley Dri. ST13 32 B4
Vicarage Rd. ST13 33 E3
Victoria St. ST13 33 F3
Wallbridge Clo. ST13 32 C5
Wallbridge Dri. ST13 32 B4
Wardle Cres. ST13 32 D5
Warrington Dri. ST13 33 F4
Waterloo St. ST13 32 D4
Well St. ST13 33 F4
Wellington St. ST13 32 D3
West End Av. ST13 32 D4
West St. ST13 32 D3
Westbourne Clo. ST13 32 C3
Westfields. ST13 33 E4
Westminster Rd. ST13 33 F2
Weston St. ST13 33 F3
Westview Clo. ST13 32 C3
Westwood Gro. ST13 32 D3
Westwood Heath Rd.
 ST13 32 C4
Westwood Park Av.
 ST13 32 B4
Westwood Park Dri.
 ST13 32 B4
Westwood Rd. ST13 32 C4
Wetenhall Dri. ST13 32 B5
Whitfield St. ST13 33 F4
Windsor Dri. ST13 33 G2
Wood St. ST13 33 F4

Woodcroft Av. ST13 32 D5
Woodcroft Rd. ST13 32 D5
Woodfield Ct. ST13 33 G3
York St. ST13 33 E3

LICHFIELD

Abbotsford Rd. WS14 35 E4
*Abnalls Ct,
 Abnalls La. WS13 34 B3
Abnalls Croft. WS13 34 B3
Abnalls La. WS13 34 A3
Alder Clo. WS14 34 B4
Andrews Ho. WS13 34 C4
Anglesey Rd. WS13 34 C2
Angorfa Clo. WS13 34 B5
Anson Av. WS13 34 C4
*Armitage Ho,
 Hobs Rd. WS13 35 F3
Ascot Clo. WS13 35 E4
*Ash Ct,
 Meadowbrook Rd.
 WS13 34 D1
Ash Gro. WS13 35 F4
Ashmole Clo. WS14 35 F5
Ashworth Ho. WS13 34 D3
Ash Tree La. WS13 35 H2
Auchinlech Dri. WS13 34 D3
Augustines Wk. WS13 34 B1
Austin Cote La. WS14 35 F4
Autumn Dri. WS13 35 E2
Backcester La. WS13 34 D4
Bailye Clo. WS13 35 G3
Bakers La. WS13 34 D4
Balmoral Clo. WS14 35 E5
Barn Clo. WS13 34 D1
Barnfield Clo. WS14 34 D5
Baskeyfield Clo. WS14 35 E4
Beacon Fields. WS13 34 C3
Beacon Gdns. WS13 34 B3
Beacon St. WS13 34 B3
Beech Gdns. WS14 34 D5
Beechfield Rise. WS14 35 E4
Beecroft Av. WS13 34 C3
Bell Clo. WS13 34 B3
Benson Clo. WS13 35 E3
Bexmore Dri. WS13 35 G3
*Birch Ct,
 Meadowbrook Rd.
 WS13 34 D1
Birch Gro. WS13 35 E4
Birchwood Rd. WS14 35 F4
Bird St. WS13 34 C4
Birmingham Rd. WS14 34 C5
Birmingham Rd. WS14 34 C6
Bishops Wk. WS13 34 C3
Blackthorne Rd. WS14 35 E4
Bloomfield Cres. WS14 34 C2
Bloomsbury Way. WS14 35 F4
Bluebird Clo. WS14 35 E4
Boley Clo. WS13 35 E4
Boley Cottage La. WS14 35 E4
Boley La. WS14 35 E4
Booth Clo. WS13 34 C2
Bore St. WS13 34 C4
Borrowcop La. WS14 34 D6
Bower Clo. WS13 35 E2
Bracken Clo. WS14 34 D6
Britannia Way. WS14 35 F5
Broad La. WS14 35 E5
Broadlands Rise. WS14 35 E5
Brook Clo. WS13 34 C3
*Brook Ct,
 Meadowbrook Rd.
 WS13 34 D1
Brownsfield Rd. WS13 35 E3
*Buckingham Gdns,
 Spencer Rd. WS14 34 D5
Bulldog La. WS13 34 C3
Burns Clo. WS14 34 C5
Burton Old Rd. WS13 35 G4
Burton Old Rd East.
 WS14 35 F4
Burton Old Rd West.
 WS13 35 E4
Burton Rd. WS13 35 F3
Byron Av. WS14 34 D6
Canterbury Clo. WS14 35 E1
Cappers La. WS13 35 F3
Carmichael Clo. WS14 35 E4
Cathedral Clo. WS14 34 C4
Cathedral Ct. WS14 34 D4
Cathedral Rise. WS13 34 C4
Cedar Clo. WS14 35 G5
*Cedar Ct,
 Meadowbrook Rd.
 WS13 34 D1
Chadwell Heights.
 WS13 35 E1

Chapel La. WS14 34 D5
Charnwood Clo. WS13 35 E3
*Charnwood Ho,
 Dimbles La. WS13 34 C2
Chaucer Clo. WS14 34 D5
Cherry Orchard. WS14 34 D5
Chester Clo. WS13 35 E1
Chesterfield Rd. WS14 34 C6
Christchurch Gdns.
 WS13 34 B4
Christchurch La. WS13 34 B4
Christopher Wk. WS13 34 C1
Church St. WS13 34 D1
*City Arc,
 Bore St. WS13 34 C4
Collins Hill. WS13 34 C2
Coltman Clo. WS14 35 E5
Conduit St. WS13 34 C4
Copper Fields. WS14 35 E4
Coppice Gro. WS14 35 G4
Cornfield Dri. WS14 35 F4
Covey Clo. WS13 35 E3
Cranefields. WS13 34 C2
Cranleigh Way. WS14 35 F4
Cricket La. WS14 35 E6
Cromwells Mdw. WS14 34 D6
Cross In Hand La.
 WS13 34 A2
Cross Keys. WS13 34 D4
Cross La. WS14 35 E5
Crossfield Rd. WS13 35 F3
Curborough Rd. WS13 34 C1
Curlew Clo. WS14 35 F5
Dam St. WS13 34 C4
Darnford La. WS13 35 F5
Darnford Moors. WS14 35 F5
Darnford View. WS13 35 F3
Darwin Clo. WS13 34 C3
*David Garrick Gdns,
 Bloomfield Cres.
 WS13 34 C1
Davidson Rd. WS14 34 D5
Deans Croft. WS13 34 A4
Dimbles Hill. WS13 34 C2
Dimbles La. WS13 34 C1
Dovehouse Fields.
 WS14 34 C6
*Drake Croft,
 Smithfield Rise. WS13 34 D3
Dyott Clo. WS13 35 G3
Eastern Av. WS13 34 A2
Elgar Clo. WS13 34 D2
Elias Clo. WS13 35 F5
*Elm Ct,
 Meadowbrook Rd.
 WS13 34 D1
Elm Gdns. WS14 34 D5
Epsom Clo. WS14 35 E4
Erasmus Way. WS13 34 B3
Essington Cres. WS14 34 C6
*Eton Ct,
 Spencer Rd. WS14 34 D5
Europa Way. WS14 35 G4
Fallow Field. WS13 34 D1
*Farm Ct,
 Meadowbrook Rd.
 WS13 34 D1
*Faulkners Yd,
 Beacon Gdns. WS13 34 B3
Featherbed La. WS13 34 A1
Fecknam Way. WS13 34 D2
Fern Croft. WS13 34 B3
Ferndale Rd. WS13 34 B2
Ferrydale Rd. WS13 34 B2
Field Rd. WS13 34 D1
Flinn Clo. WS13 35 E5
Forge La. WS13 34 B3
*Forrest Ct,
 Birmingham Rd.
 WS13 34 C5
Fossway. WS14 34 C5
Foxgloves Clo. WS14 34 C1
Francis Rd. WS13 34 C6
Freeford Gdns. WS14 35 F5
Frenchmans Wk. WS13 34 C5
Friars All. WS13 34 C4
Friary Av. WS13 34 C5
Friary Gdns. WS13 34 B5
Friary Rd. WS14 34 C5
Friday Acre. WS13 34 C3
Frog La. WS13 34 D4
Furnival Cres. WS13 35 E3
Gable Croft. WS14 34 D6
Gaia La. WS13 34 C3
Gaiafields Rd. WS13 34 C2
Gaialands Cres. WS13 34 C2
Gaiastowe. WS13 34 D3
Garrick Clo. WS13 34 B2
Garrick Rd. WS13 34 B4
George La. WS13 34 D4
Giffords Cft. WS13 34 B3

Gilbert Rd. WS13 35 E2
Gilbert Wk. WS13 35 E2
Giles Rd. WS13 34 C1
Gledhill Pk. WS14 34 D6
Gloucester Clo. WS13 34 D1
Goodwood Clo. WS14 35 E4
Gorse La. WS14 35 E5
Gorsty Bank. WS13 35 F4
Grange La. WS13 34 A1
*Green Ct,
 Birmingham Rd
 . WS13 34 D5
Greencroft. WS13 34 B2
Greenhough Rd. WS13 34 B3
Greenwood Dri. WS14 34 D5
Gresley Row. WS13 34 D4
Grosvenor Clo. WS14 35 E5
*Guardian Ho,
 Rotten Row. WS13 34 D4
Handel Wk. WS13 34 D2
Hartslade. WS14 35 F5
Harwood Rd. WS13 34 D4
Havefield Av. WS13 35 F4
Hawkesmoor Dri.
 WS14 35 E4
Hawkins Clo. WS13 34 C2
Hawthorne Clo. WS13 34 E4
*Hawthorne Ho,
 Hawthorne Clo. WS14 35 E4
Hayes Vw. WS13 34 B3
Haymoor. WS14 35 F5
Hayworth Clo. WS13 34 D2
Hazel Gro. WS14 34 D5
Heenan Gro. WS13 34 B2
Henderson Clo. WS14 35 E4
*Henley Ct,
 Spencer Rd. WS14 34 D5
Heritage Ct. WS14 35 E5
Hermes Rd. WS13 35 E2
Hewit Clo. WS13 34 C2
*Highcroft Cres,
 Hazel Gro. WS14 34 D5
Highfield Gdns. WS13 34 F5
Hillcrest Dri. WS13 34 C3
Hillside. WS14 34 C3
Hobs Rd. WS13 35 F3
Holland Clo. WS13 35 G2
Holywell Rise. WS14 35 E5
*Houlbrooke Ho,
 Lunns Croft. WS13 34 D3
Hunter Clo. WS13 35 E6
INDUSTRIAL & RETAIL:
Britannia Enterprise Pk.
 WS14 35 G3
City Wharf Ind Est.
 WS14 34 D4
Greenhough Trading Est.
 WS13 34 B3
Lichfield Business Pk.
 SW13 35 F2
Shires Ind Est. WS14 34 C6
Trent Valley Ind Est.
 WS13 35 E2
Windsor Business Pk.
 WS13 35 F3
Irving Clo. WS13 34 A2
Ivanhoe Rd. WS14 34 C5
Jackson Rd. WS13 34 D1
James Green Way.
 WS13 34 C2
Johnson Clo. WS13 35 E2
Jordon Clo. WS13 34 C3
Jude Wk. WS13 34 B2
Kean Clo. WS13 34 A2
Keepers Clo. WS14 35 F5
Kenilworth Rd. WS14 34 D5
Kings Hill Rd. WS14 34 D6
Kings Mews. WS14 34 C6
Laburnum Ct. WS14 34 C6
Lambourne Clo. WS14 35 F4
Langton Ct. WS14 34 B3
Larch Clo. WS14 35 F5
Laurel Clo. WS13 34 E4
Lawford Av. WS14 35 F4
Leomansley Clo. WS13 34 B4
Leomansley Rd. WS13 34 A5
Leomansley Vw. WS13 34 A5
Leomansley Ct. WS13 34 A5
Levetts Field. WS13 34 F4
Lewis Clo. WS14 34 C6
Leyfields. WS13 34 C2
Lichfield Pk. WS13 34 C3
Lillington Clo. WS14 34 C3
Lime Gro. WS14 34 D6
Lincoln Clo. WS13 34 D1
Little Barrow Wk. WS13 34 C3
Little Grange. WS13 34 B2
Lomax Clo. WS13 34 D4
Lombard St. WS13 34 D4
Long Bridge Rd. WS14 34 D6
Longstaff Croft. WS13 34 B2

Lower Sandford St.
 WS13 34
*Lukes Wk,
 James Green Way.
 WS13 34
Lunns Croft. WS13 34
Lyn Av. WS13 34
Lynfield Rd. WS13 34
*Mallard Croft,
 Smithfield Rise. WS13 34
Mallicot Clo. WS13 35
Manley Rd. WS13 35
Manor Rise. WS14 35
*Maple Ct,
 Laburnum Ct. WS14 34
Maple Gro. WS14 34
Market St. WS13 34
Marks Wk. WS13 34
Marlborough Ct. WS13 34
Marsh La. WS14 34
Martin Croft. WS13 34
Mary Vale Ct. WS13 34
Masefield Clo. WS14 34
Matthews Wk. WS13 34
Mawgan Dri. WS14 35
Maxwell Clo. WS13 34
Maybank Clo. WS14 34
*Meadowbrook Rd.
 WS13 34
Meadow Croft. WS13 35
Mesnes Grn. WS14 35
*Mill Ct,
 Meadowbrook Rd.
 WS13 34
Minors Hill. WS14 34
Nearfield Ho. WS13 34
Needwood Hill. WS13 34
Nether Beacon. WS13 34
Netherbridge Av. WS14 35
Netherstowe. WS13 34
Netherstowe La. WS13 34
Newlyn Clo. WS13 34
Newton Rd. WS13 34
Norwich Clo. WS13 34
Nursery Croft. WS13 34
Oakenfield. WS13 34
Oakhurst. WS14 34
Oakley Clo. WS13 34
Old Rd. WS14 34
Orchard Clo. WS13 35
Paget Clo. WS13 34
Park End. WS14 34
Partridge Croft. WS13 34
Pauls Wk. WS13 34
*Pennys Croft,
 Hobs Rd. WS13 35
Pentire Rd. WS14 35
Peters Wk. WS13 34
Pinfold Rd. WS13 34
Pipers Croft. WS13 34
Ploughmans Wk. WS13 34
Pones Grn. WS13 34
Ponesfield Rd. WS13 34
Pool Wk. WS13 34
*Pourbaix Ho,
 Birmingham Rd.
 WS13 34
*Prince Ruperts Mews,
 Beacon St. WS13 34
Prince Ruperts Way.
 WS13 34
Prospect Dri. WS14 35
Purcell Av. WS13 34
Quarry Hills La. WS14 35
Queen St. WS13 34
*Quonians La,
 Dam St. WS13 34
Redlock Field. WS14 34
Reeves La. WS13 34
Reynolds Clo. WS13 34
Richmond Dri. WS14 35
*Ridware Ho,
 Hobs Rd. WS13 35
Rocklands Cres. WS13 35
Roman Way. WS14 34
Romilly Clo. WS13 34
*Rookery Ct,
 Leomansley Vw.
 WS13 34
Rotten Row. WS13 34
Rowan Clo. WS13 34
Ryknild St. WS13 34
St Annes Rd. WS13 34
St Catherines Rd. WS13 34
St Chads Clo. WS13 34
*St Chads Ct,
 Cross Keys. WS13 34
St Chads Rd. WS13 34
St John St. WS13 34
St Johns Clo. WS13 34
St Margarets Rd. WS13 34
St Marys Rd. WS13 34

Michael Rd. WS13 34 D3
isbury Clo. WS13 34 D1
nuel Clo. WS13 34 D2
idford Ho. WS13 34 C4
idford St. WS13 34 C4
axon Ct,
Leomansley Vw.
WS13 34 A5
xon Wk. WS13 34 A5
otch Orchard. WS13 35 E3
ott Clo. WS14 34 C5
ckham Rd. WS13 34 B3
ward Clo. WS14 35 E6
akespeare Av. WS14 34 D5
nenstone Ho,
Hobs Rd. WS13 35 F3
apherds Clo. WS13 34 D1
eriffs Clo. WS14 35 F5
ortbutts La. WS14 34 C6
dons Clo. WS13 34 B2
npson Rd. WS13 34 D1
tall Ridge. WS13 34 B2
iithfield Rise. WS13 34 D3
ithy La. WS13 34 B3
uthern Cross. WS13 34 D4
uthwark Clo. WS13 34 D1
earhill. WS14 35 F4
encer Rd. WS14 34 D5
ring Gro. WS13 35 E2
fford Rd. WS13 34 A2
fford St. WS13 34 A1
tion Rd. WS13 34 D4
phens Wk. WS13 34 B1
venson Wk. WS14 34 C5
towe Ct,
Stow St. WS13 34 D4
towe Hill Gdns,
Johnson Clo. WS13 35 E2
we Rd. WS13 34 D3
we St. WS13 34 D3
wecroft. WS13 34 D4
rgeons Hill. WS14 35 E4
chbrook Gdns.
WS13 34 D2
llivan Way. WS13 35 E2
nmer Gro. WS13 35 E2
nbury Av. WS13 35 F4
allow Cft. WS13 34 B3
an Mews. WS13 34 C4
an Rd. WS13 34 C4
infen Broun Rd.
WS13 34 B3
nworth Rd. WS13 34 D6
nworth St. WS13 34 D4
nyard. WS13 34 D3
arnet Ho,
Frog La. WS13 34 D4
ry Clo. WS13 34 A2
e Brambles. WS14 35 E5
e Charters. WS13 34 D3
e Chequers. WS13 34 D3
e Crossing. WS14 35 F4
e Dell. WS13 34 B4
e Dimbles. WS13 34 C1
e Friary. WS13 34 C4
e Garth. WS13 34 C2
e Grange. WS13 34 B2
ne Hedgerows,
Shortbutts La. WS14 34 C6
e Leasowe. WS13 34 D4
e Paddock. WS14 34 D6
e Parchments. WS13 34 D3
e Pines. WS14 35 F4
e Spires. WS14 35 F5
e Squirrels. WS14 35 E4
e Sycamores. WS14 34 C6
e Windings. WS13 34 C3
e Woodlands. WS13 35 E3
stley Nook. WS13 34 C2
omas Green Way.
WS13 34 B2
an Way. WS13 35 G4
vnfields. WS13 34 C4
vnfields. WS13 34 C4
gony Rise. WS14 35 E5
nance Clo. WS14 35 E5
nt Valley. WS13 35 F3
nt Valley Rd. WS13 35 E4
ro Clo. WS13 34 D1
ador Row,
Wade St. WS13 34 C4
e Clo. WS13 34 B3
per St John St. WS14 34 C4
ley La. WS13 35 E3
di Ct. WS13 34 D2
ars Clo. WS13 34 C4
toria Gdns. WS13 34 B5
can Rd. WS13 35 F3
de St. WS13 34 C4
lkers Croft. WS13 34 D6
nut Gro. WS14 35 G5
nsall Rd. WS13 34 A5

Warren Clo. WS14 35 F5
Waverley Wk. WS14 34 C5
Wellington Pl. WS14 34 C6
Wentworth Dri. WS14 34 C5
Western By-Pass. WS13 34 A2
Weston Rd. WS13 34 B2
Wharf Clo. WS13 34 D5
Wheel La. WS13 34 B3
*Whittington Ho,
Hobs Rd. WS13 35 F3
Wightman Clo. WS14 35 F5
*Willow Ct,
Laburnum Ct. WS14 34 D6
Willow Tree Clo. WS13 34 C2
Willowsmere Dri. WS14 35 E6
Wilmot Clo. WS13 34 B4
*Wiltell Lodge,
Wiltell Rd. WS14 34 D5
Wiltell Rd. WS14 34 D5
Winchester Clo. WS13 34 D1
Windmill Clo. WS13 34 B2
Windmill La. WS13 34 B2
*Windsor Ct,
Spencer Rd. WS14 34 D5
Winter Clo. WS13 35 E2
Wissage Ct. WS13 35 E4
*Wissage Croft,
St Chads Rd. WS13 34 D3
Wissage La. WS13 35 E3
Wissage Rd. WS13 35 E3
Wolsey Rd. WS13 34 D4
Wood Ridings. WS14 34 C2
Woodfields Dri. WS14 35 F6
Woods Croft. WS13 34 C3
Worcester Clo. WS13 34 D1
Wordsworth Clo. WS14 34 D6
Wyrley Clo. WS14 34 C6
Yale Clo. WS13 34 C3
Yew Tree Av. WS14 35 F4
York Clo. WS13 35 E1

LONGTON

Addington Way. ST3 36 C2
Albert Av. ST3 36 D5
Albert St. ST3 36 B2
Alberta St. ST3 36 B6
Alexandra Rd. ST3 36 D6
Allensmore Av. ST4 36 A2
Almer St. ST3 36 C4
Althrop Gro. ST3 36 C4
Amberfield Clo. ST3 36 D4
Amblecote Dri. ST3 36 D4
Amison St. ST3 36 B3
Anchor Pl. ST3 36 B3
Anchor Rd. ST3 36 B4
Anchor Ter. ST3 36 B4
Andover Clo. ST3 36 B1
Annette Rd. ST4 36 A1
Anthony Pl. ST3 36 C3
Argyll Rd. ST3 36 C6
Arundel Way. ST3 36 B1
Asherwood Pl. ST3 36 C4
Ashridge Gro. ST3 36 C1
Ashwood. ST4 36 A2
*Ashwood Ter,
Ashwood. ST3 36 A2
Auden Pl. ST3 36 C4
Ayshford Clo. ST3 36 A5
Bambury St. ST3 36 B1
Barbrook Av. ST3 36 D4
Barclay St. ST4 36 A2
Barford St. ST3 36 A4
Barker St. ST3 36 B5
Barleyford Dri. ST3 36 C1
Barlow St. ST3 36 C2
Bartlem St. ST3 36 C2
Baths Pass. ST3 36 A4
Baths Rd. ST3 36 A3
Bathurst St. ST3 36 B4
Battison Cres. ST3 36 A6
Beaufort Rd. ST3 36 B5
Beech St. ST3 36 B4
Beeston St. ST3 36 B2
Belgrave Av. ST3 36 A6
Belgrave Rd. ST3 36 A6
Belsay Clo. ST3 36 A3
Bengry Rd. ST3 36 D6
Bennet Precinct. ST3 36 B5
Bennion St. ST3 36 B5
Berry La. ST3 36 A4
Blackheath Clo. ST3 36 C5
Blantyre St. ST3 36 A6
Bosinney Clo. ST4 36 A2
Branson Av. ST3 36 B4
Brickfield Pl. ST3 36 B1
Bridgewood St. ST3 36 B1
Brightgates St. ST3 36 C1
Brockford St. ST4 36 A2

Buccleuch Rd. ST3 36 C6
Bywater Gro. ST3 36 C1
Calverley St. ST3 36 C5
Capewell St. ST3 36 B3
Caroline St. ST3 36 A4
Carroll Dri. ST3 36 A4
Carron St. ST4 36 A2
Castledine Gro. ST3 36 C3
Cemetery Av. ST3 36 A6
Cemetery Vw. ST3 36 A5
Chadwick St. ST3 36 B5
Chancery La. ST3 36 A4
Chaplin Rd. ST3 36 B6
Chatfield Pl. ST3 36 C5
Chatterton Pl. ST3 36 C4
Checkley Gro. ST3 36 C1
Chelson St. ST3 36 B6
Chepstow Pl. ST3 36 B1
Church Gdns. ST3 36 A3
Cinderhill La. ST3 36 D5
Clarence Rd. ST3 36 A3
Clayfield Gro. ST3 36 A1
Clewlow Pl. ST3 36 B5
Clivedon Pl. ST3 36 B5
Commerce St. ST3 36 C3
Conrad Clo. ST3 36 C4
Copperstone Gro. ST3 36 D1
Corfe Grn. ST3 36 B1
Corina Way. ST3 36 C3
Cornwall St. ST3 36 B3
Coronation Av. ST3 36 A4
Cottonwood Gro. ST3 36 D1
Court No. 1. ST3 36 D6
Cromartie St. ST3 36 B6
Deanscroft Way. ST3 36 D4
Delwood Gro. ST3 36 C1
Denby Av. ST3 36 A2
Dobell Gro. ST3 36 C3
Drayton Rd. ST3 36 A3
Dunrobin St. ST3 36 B6
Dunster Rd. ST3 36 A6
Dylan Rd. ST3 36 C4
Edensor Rd. ST3 36 B5
Edgar Pl. ST3 36 B1
Edgefield Rd. ST3 36 B2
Ely Walk. ST3 36 B3
Erskine St. ST3 36 B6
Eversley Rd. ST3 36 B6
Evesham Way. ST3 36 D4
Farmer St. ST3 36 B5
Farnworth Dri. ST3 36 D4
Fern Pl. ST3 36 A6
Field Pl. ST3 36 B2
Fistral Clo. ST3 36 A2
Flackett St. ST3 36 B3
Fleckney Av. ST3 36 A5
Fleur Gro. ST3 36 A1
Forrister St. ST3 36 B3
Forsythe Rd. ST3 36 A1
Freebridge Clo. ST3 36 D3
Friar St. ST3 36 B4
Furnace Rd. ST3 36 C6
Garsworthy Rd. ST3 36 A1
Gawsworth Clo. ST3 36 C1
George Ct. ST3 36 A4
Glenwood Clo. ST3 36 B3
Goddard St. ST3 36 B4
Gold St. ST3 36 B4
Goldenhill Rd. ST3 36 A3
Goldsmith Pl. ST3 36 C4
Gower St. ST3 36 B5
Grafton Rd. ST3 36 A3
Greendock St. ST3 36 A5
Hackett Clo. ST3 36 B4
Haggett Gro. ST3 36 B6
Haig St. ST3 36 C5
Hamilton Rd. ST3 36 C6
Harber St. ST3 36 B4
Hardsacre Rd. ST3 36 C2
Hathersage Clo. ST3 36 B1
Heath Pass. ST3 36 B5
Heathcote Rd. ST3 36 A4
Heathcote St. ST3 36 A1
Heathdene Clo. ST3 36 A3
Heber St. ST3 36 D4
Helston Av. ST3 36 D4
Hemingway Rd. ST3 36 B5
Hemlock Pl. ST3 36 B3
Hillgreen Rd. ST3 36 C1
Holmesfield Walk. ST3 36 B6
Honiton Walk. ST3 36 B6
Howard St. ST3 36 A6
Hudson Walk. ST3 36 B4
Huxley Pl. ST3 36 C4
Imogen Clo. ST3 36 C4
Jade St. ST3 36 C3
Jervison St. ST3 36 B3
Jolyon Clo. ST4 36 A1
June Rd. ST4 36 A1
Kelnore Gro. ST3 36 A3
Kendrick St. ST3 36 C4

Kentmere Clo. ST4 36 A2
Kildare St. ST3 36 B6
King St. ST4 36 A3
Kingcross St. ST3 36 A4
Kirkbridge Clo. ST3 36 C3
Knarsdale Clo. ST3 36 C2
Lamotte Clo. ST4 36 A2
Landon St. ST3 36 B4
Larkin Av. ST3 36 C3
Lawley St. ST3 36 C5
Leaks All. ST3 36 A5
Ledstone Way. ST3 36 D4
Lennox Rd. ST3 36 C6
Leveson St. ST3 36 B6
Lightwood Rd. ST3 36 A5
Lilleshall St. ST3 36 B6
Linnburn Rd. ST3 36 B5
Lloyd St. ST3 36 B6
Locketts La. ST3 36 B6
Loganbeck Gro. ST3 36 D2
Longley Rd. ST3 36 A2
Longsdon Gro. ST3 36 D4
Longview Clo. ST3 36 C2
Loughborough Wk. ST3 36 D4
Loveston Gro. ST3 36 D4
Lower Spring Rd. ST3 36 C5
Ludbrook Rd. ST4 36 A2
Malt La. ST3 36 C5
Mandella Way. ST3 36 B6
Manse Clo. ST3 36 B3
March Rd. ST3 36 A3
Market St. ST3 36 A4
Marlborough Rd. ST3 36 A3
Marlow Clo. ST3 36 C2
Marlow Rd. ST3 36 C2
May Pl. ST4 36 A3
Meir Rd. ST3 36 D6
Meirhay Rd. ST3 36 C5
Melbourne St. ST3 36 C2
Melville Rd. ST3 36 D6
Menai Gro. ST3 36 B2
Merton St. ST3 36 B3
Mid Cross St. ST3 36 B3
Millbank St. ST3 36 B4
Monty St. ST3 36 A1
Morpeth St. ST3 36 B5
Mossfield Rd. ST3 36 C6
Mossland Rd. ST3 36 B2
Moulton Rd. ST3 36 A4
Naples Clo. ST3 36 D3
Neath Clo. ST3 36 B1
Neath Pl. ST3 36 B1
New Hall Rd. ST3 36 D5
Newmount Rd. ST4 36 A1
Normacot Rd. ST3 36 B5
Normanton Gro. ST3 36 C1
Nyewood Av. ST3 36 B1
Olaf Palm Gro. ST3 36 B6
Oldway Pl. ST3 36 B2
Packett St. ST4 36 A3
Paragon Rd. ST3 36 B4
Park Hall Rd. ST3 36 D2
Park Hall St. ST3 36 B3
Pendine Gro. ST3 36 A1
Pevensey Gro. ST3 36 B1
Pinhoe Pl. ST3 36 D4
Pitlea Pl. ST3 36 B1
Pitsford St. ST3 36 B3
Plant St. ST3 36 B3
Portland Rd. ST3 36 C6
Priestley Dri. ST3 36 C3
Priorfield Clo. ST3 36 A3
Probyn Ct. ST3 36 A6
Queensbury Rd. ST3 36 C6
Rachel Gro. ST4 36 A1
Railway Pas. ST3 36 B4
Railway Ter. ST3 36 C4
Ramshaw Gro. ST3 36 C1
Recreation Rd. ST3 36 D6
Reservoir Rd. ST3 36 A3
Rill St. ST4 36 A3
Rimini Clo. ST3 36 D2
Robin Hill Gro. ST4 36 A2
Rochester Rd. ST3 36 A2
Rogate Clo. ST4 36 A1
Ronald St. ST3 36 B6
Rosslyn Rd. ST3 36 B5
Rothesay Rd. ST3 36 C6
Rowandale Clo. ST3 36 D4
Roxburghe Av. ST3 36 B6
Royston Walk. ST3 36 B4
Ruskin Clo. ST3 36 C3
Rustington Av. ST3 36 D4
Rutland Rd. ST3 36 A3
St Clair St. ST3 36 B6
St Martins La. ST3 36 A4
St Marys Rd. ST3 36 D6
Saltdean Clo. ST3 36 D6
Sandford St. ST3 36 B3
Sandgate St. ST3 36 C5
Sandwood Cres. ST3 36 B2

Sark Pl. ST3 36 C1
Sedgley Walk. ST3 36 B4
Sefton Rd. ST3 36 D6
Sheaf Pass. ST3 36 B5
Sheldrake Gro. ST4 36 A1
Shenton St. ST3 36 C2
Short Banbury St.
ST3 36 C1
Short St. ST3 36 B5
Sitwell Gro. ST3 36 C3
Skye Clo. ST3 36 D4
Smith St. ST3 36 B3
Smithy La. ST3 36 B4
Soames Cres. ST3 36 A1
Solway Gro. ST3 36 D4
Somerton Way. ST3 36 C2
Sorrento Gro. ST3 36 D3
Souldern Way. ST3 36 C3
Speakman St. ST3 36 C6
Speedwall St. ST3 36 B2
Spratslade Dri. ST3 36 A6
Spring Garden Rd. ST3 36 A5
Spring Garden Ter. ST3 36 A5
Spring Rd. ST3 36 D6
Springfield Cres. ST3 36 A4
Stafford St. ST3 36 A4
Stanfield St. ST3 36 C1
Stockwell Gro. ST3 36 C5
Summer Row. ST3 36 A5
Sutherland Av. ST3 36 A6
Sutherland Rd. ST3 36 B4
Swanland Gro. ST3 36 C3
Swithen Dri. ST4 36 A1
Tatton St. ST3 36 B6
Tay Clo. ST3 36 A2
The Strand. ST3 36 A4
Thirlmere Gro. ST3 36 D5
Tideswell Rd. ST3 36 B2
Times Sq. ST3 36 D4
Transport La. ST3 36 A4
Trentham Rd. ST3 36 A6
Tunnicliffe Clo. ST3 36 D5
Tuscan St. ST3 36 B3
Tutbury Clo. ST3 36 C3
Upper Cross St. ST3 36 B3
Upper Normacot Rd.
ST3 36 C6
Uttoxeter Rd. ST3 36 B4
Verona Gro. ST3 36 D2
Vienna Way. ST3 36 D2
Walmer Pl. ST3 36 A1
Walpole St. ST3 36 C2
Warren Pl. ST3 36 C5
Warren St. ST3 36 B5
Warsill Gro. ST3 36 C3
Waterdale Gro. ST3 36 D4
Webberley La. ST3 36 B5
Weston Coyney Rd. ST3 36 C5
Weston St. ST3 36 C1
Westonview Av. ST3 36 C2
Westsprink Cres. ST3 36 D6
Wigmore Pl. ST3 36 B1
Willow Row. ST3 36 A5
Wilmot Gro. ST3 36 C6
Windsor Av. ST3 36 C6
Winterbourne Gro. ST3 36 D4
Woddingdean Clo. ST3 36 D4
Wolstern Rd. ST3 36 C1
Wood St. ST3 36 A3
Worth Clo. ST3 36 C3
Wren Vw. ST3 36 C6
Yarmouth Walk. ST3 36 C2

MADELEY

Agger Hill. CW3 37 F1
Apple Croft. CW3 37 B2
Arbour Clo. CW3 37 A4
Barhill Rd. CW3 37 A4
Beck Rd. CW3 37 C2
Beech Croft. CW3 37 C2
Beresford Dale. CW3 37 B3
Bevan Pl. CW3 37 C3
Birch Dale. CW3 37 B3
Birch Mews. CW3 37 B3
Bower End La. CW3 37 B4
Boysey Wood Rd. CW3 37 B1
Bramble Lea. CW3 37 C3
Castle La. CW3 37 C4
Charles Cotton Dri.
CW3 37 B3
Cherry Hill. CW3 37 B3
College Clo. CW3 37 C2
Corrie Clo. CW3 37 C4
Cygnet Clo. CW3 37 C1
Daltry Way. CW3 37 C2
Elkington Rise. CW3 37 B3
Fern Dene. CW3 37 B2
Furnace La. CW3 37 A2

Garners Walk. CW3 37 C2
Grayling Willows. CW3 37 C3
Greenmeadows Rd. CW3
Heath Row. CW3 37 E1
Heather Glade. CW3 37 B2
Heighley Castle Way. CW3 37 C1
Heron Clo. CW3 37 C2
Hidden Hill. CW3 37 C1
Hillwood Rd. CW3 37 E1
Holm Oak Dri. CW3 37 C2
Honeywall La. CW3 37 F2
Hungerford La. CW3 37 C4
Izaac Walton Way. CW3 37 B4
John Offley Rd. CW3 37 B3
Keele Rd. CW3 37 D1
Kingfisher Clo. CW3 37 D2
Knightley. CW3 37 C4
Laverock Gro. CW3 37 B4
Leycett La. CW3 37 F1
Lindops La. CW3 37 C2
Lynam Way. CW3 37 C2
Manor La. CW3 37 B4
Merlin Grn. CW3 37 B3
Mill La. CW3 37 C2
Monument View. CW3 37 E2
Morningside. CW3 37 B3
Moss La. CW3 37 B3
Netherset Hey La. CW3 37 C4
New Rd. CW3 37 C2
Newcastle Rd. CW3 37 C3
Park Clo. CW3 37 C1
Parkside. CW3 37 D2
Pastoral Clo. CW3 37 C4
Pear Tree Dri. CW3 37 B3
Plover Field. CW3 37 B3
Poolside. CW3 37 C3
Primrose Dell. CW3 37 B3
Red La. CW3 37 B4
River Lea Mews. CW3 37 B3
Roseberry Dri. CW3 37 C2
Salisbury Clo. CW3 37 C2
Sawpit Yard. CW3 37 D2
Station Rd. CW3 37 C4
The Bridle Path. CW3 37 B2
The Holborn. CW3 37 C4
The Spinney. CW3 37 E1
Thornhill Dri. CW3 37 C2
Vicarage La. CW3 37 C4
Watering Trough Bank. CW3 37 F2
Waterside Clo. CW3 37 C3
Wharf Ter. CW3 37 E1
Woodland Hill. CW3 37 C1
Woodside. CW3 37 C3
Works Dri. CW3 37 E2

NEWCASTLE-UNDER-LYME

Abbots Way. ST5 38 B6
Albany Rd. ST5 38 B2
Albemarle Rd. ST5 38 A1
Andrew Pl. ST5 38 D3
Ashfields New Rd. ST5 38 B2
Baden St. ST5 38 B2
Bailey St. ST5 38 B3
Balcombe Clo. ST5 38 B5
Balls Yd. ST5 38 C3
Bankside. ST5 38 D4
Barracks Rd. ST5 38 C1
Beattie Av. ST5 38 C1
Beaumaris Ct. ST5 38 A5
Belgrave Rd. ST5 38 D4
Beresford Cres. ST5 38 A6
Blackfriars Rd. ST5 38 D3
Borough Rd. ST5 38 D3
Brackenberry. ST5 38 C1
Bramfield Dri. ST5 38 C2
Brampton Gdns. ST5 38 D1
Brampton Rd. ST5 38 D2
Brampton Sidings. ST5 38 C2
Bridge St. ST5 38 B3
Brindley St. ST5 38 C3
Broad St. ST5 38 C3
Brook La. ST5 38 C5
Brookside Clo. ST5 38 A5
Brunswick St. ST5 38 B3
Buckleys Row. ST5 38 B4
Buckmaster Av. ST5 38 D6
Castle Hill Rd. ST5 38 B3
*Castle Keep Mews,
    Silverdale Rd. ST5 38 A3
Castle Ridge. ST5 38 A4
Castle St. ST5 38 D3
Chantry Rd. ST5 38 D1
Charter Rd. ST5 38 B1
Cheapside. ST5 38 C4

Church St. ST5 38 B3
Clarence St. ST5 38 D3
Clayton Rd. ST5 38 C5
Coronation Rd. ST5 38 D4
Corporation St. ST5 38 C3
Croft Rd. ST5 38 C2
Cross May St. ST5 38 B4
Cumberland St. ST5 38 D3
Deansgate. ST5 38 A4
Delamere Gro. ST5 38 C2
Dene Side. ST5 38 A4
Douglas Rd. ST5 38 A1
Drayton St. ST5 38 B4
Duke St. ST5 38 D5
Dunkirk. ST5 38 B3
Dunkirk Ct. ST5 38 B3
Earl St. ST5 38 D3
Earls Ct. ST5 38 D3
Eleanor Cres. ST5 38 B6
Eleanor Pl. ST5 38 B6
Emery Av. ST5 38 A5
Enderley St. ST5 38 B2
Fairlawns. ST5 38 C1
Fletcher Bank. ST5 38 C3
Florence St. ST5 38 C3
Fogg St. ST5 38 C3
Freehold St. ST5 38 D4
Friars St. ST5 38 B4
Friars Walk. ST5 38 B6
Friarswood Rd. ST5 38 B4
Froghall. ST5 38 B3
Garden St. ST5 38 C4
George St. ST5 38 D3
Goodwin Av. ST5 38 B1
Goose St. ST5 38 C4
Gower St. ST5 38 D3
Granville Av. ST5 38 D2
Greenbook Ct. ST5 38 C1
Greenside. ST5 38 B3
Grosvenor Gdns. ST5 38 D4
Grosvenor Rd. ST5 38 C4
Hall St. ST5 38 B3
Hanover St. ST5 38 C3
Harrison St. ST5 38 D5
Hart Ct. ST5 38 B3
Hassam Av. ST5 38 B1
Hassell St. ST5 38 C4
Hatrell St. ST5 38 C5
Hawkstone Clo. ST5 38 D5
Heath Av. ST5 38 C1
Heath St. ST5 38 C3
Hedley Pl. ST5 38 A4
Hempstalls La. ST5 38 C2
Hick St. ST5 38 C4
Hickman St. ST5 38 B3
High St. ST5 38 C3
Higherland. ST5 38 A4
Highfield Ct. ST5 38 C6
Hill St. ST5 38 B2
Hillside. ST5 38 A5
Holborn. ST5 38 B3
Honeywood. ST5 38 C1
Howard Gro. ST5 38 A6
Howards Pl. ST5 38 A6
Hughes Av. ST5 38 B1
Hyacinth Ct. ST5 38 C1
INDUSTRIAL & RETAIL:
Brampton Ind Est.
    ST5 38 B2
Ironmarket. ST5 38 C3
Jason St. ST5 38 B2
Jenkinson Clo. ST5 38 A5
John O'Gaunts Rd. ST5 38 B3
Kimberley Grange. ST5 38 C1
Kimberley Rd. ST5 38 B1
King St. ST5 38 C3
Knutton La. ST5 38 A2
Lad La. ST5 38 C3
Lancaster Av. ST5 38 D4
Lancaster Rd. ST5 38 D4
Larkspur Gro. ST5 38 C1
Laxey Rd. ST5 38 A1
Leech St. ST5 38 D5
Legge St. ST5 38 D5
Liverpool Rd. ST5 38 B1
London Rd. ST5 38 C4
Lower St. ST5 38 B3
Lyme Valley Rd. ST5 38 C5
Lyme Wood Gro. ST5 38 B5
Lymewood Clo. ST5 38 B5
Marina Dri. ST5 38 D1
Market La. ST5 38 C2
Marsh Par. ST5 38 D3
May Pl. ST5 38 D1
Mayer Av. ST5 38 B1
Mayfield Av. ST5 38 A4
Mellard St. ST5 38 C2
Merrial St. ST5 38 C3
Milford Rd. ST5 38 A5
Mill St. ST5 38 B2
Miller St. ST5 38 D3

Montfort Pl. ST5 38 C6
Moran Rd. ST5 38 A2
Mount Pleasant. ST5 38 D4
Myott Av. ST5 38 B5
Nelson Pl. ST5 38 C3
North St. ST5 38 D3
Northcote Pl. ST5 38 D3
Occupation St. ST5 38 D5
Orion Ct. ST5 38 A4
Orme Rd. ST5 38 A3
Orton Rd. ST5 38 B1
Paradise St. ST5 38 C4
Parkstone Av. ST5 38 D5
Pembroke Dri. ST5 38 A5
Penarth Pl. ST5 38 A5
Pepper St. ST5 38 C4
Pilkington Av. ST5 38 B6
Pool Dam. ST5 38 B4
Pool Side. ST5 38 B3
Pool St. ST5 38 B4
Poolfield Av. ST5 38 A4
Poplar Gro. ST5 38 D3
Primrose Gro. ST5 38 C1
Princess St. ST5 38 D3
Priory Rd. ST5 38 B6
Prospect Ter. ST5 38 B3
Pump St. ST5 38 B4
Queen St. ST5 38 C3
Queens Ct. ST5 38 C3
Ramsey Rd. ST5 38 A1
Roberts Av. ST5 38 B1
Ronaldsway Dri. ST5 38 A1
Roseacre. ST5 38 A5
Rotterdam. ST5 38 A3
Rye Bank. ST5 38 C3
Rye Bank Cres. ST5 38 C3
Ryecroft. ST5 38 B3
St Andrews Dri. ST5 38 A4
St Anthonys Dri. ST5 38 A6
St Georges Rd. ST5 38 A4
St Martins Rd. ST5 38 A4
St Marys Dri. ST5 38 A4
St Michaels Rd. ST5 38 B1
St Pauls Rd. ST5 38 A3
Sandy La. ST5 38 D1
School St. ST5 38 C3
Seabridge Rd. ST5 38 B6
Seagrave St. ST5 38 D3
Shaw St. ST5 38 C3
Sidmouth Av. ST5 38 D2
Silverdale Rd. ST5 38 A3
Slaney St. ST5 38 D5
Sneyd Av. ST5 38 A6
Sneyd Cres. ST5 38 A6
Stanier St. ST5 38 B3
Station Walk. ST5 38 C2
Stubbs Gate. ST5 38 C5
Stubbs St. ST5 38 C4
Stubbs Walk. ST5 38 D4
Stubbsfield Rd. ST5 38 D5
Sunny Hollow. ST5 38 D1
The Avenue. ST5 38 D5
The Briars. ST5 38 C1
The Crescent. ST5 38 B6
The Grove. ST5 38 C6
The Hollies. ST5 38 D2
The Midway. ST5 38 B4
The Parkway. ST5 38 B6
Thistleberry Av. ST5 38 A5
Thistleberry Villas. ST5 38 A5
Tulip Gro. ST5 38 C2
Tynwald Grange. ST5 38 D4
Vessey Ter. ST5 38 D4
Vicarage Cres. ST5 38 D5
Victoria Rd. ST5 38 D4
Victoria St. ST5 38 D5
Water St. ST5 38 D3
Webster St. ST5 38 D5
Wedgwood Av. ST5 38 A6
Well St. ST5 38 C4
Wesley Pl. ST5 38 A4
West Brampton. ST5 38 D2
West St. ST5 38 D4
Westlands Av. ST5 38 A5
Wharf St. ST5 38 D3
Whitfield Av. ST5 38 A5
Whitmore Rd. ST5 38 A6
Wilson St. ST5 38 C2
Wilton St. ST5 38 B1
Woodstock Clo. ST5 38 B1
Wulstan Dri. ST5 38 C1
York Pl. ST5 38 C3
York St. ST5 38 D3

PENKRIDGE

Abbey Clo. ST19 39 C2
Ablon Ct. ST19 39 D1
Aston Clo. ST19 39 D3

Bartlett Clo. ST19 39 C2
Bedingstone Dri. ST19 39 D3
Bellbrook. ST19 39 B1
Beverley Clo. ST19 39 C3
Bitham Clo. ST19 39 C3
Blount Clo. ST19 39 C3
Boscomoor Ct. ST19 39 B3
Boscomoor Clo. ST19 39 B3
Boscomoor La. ST19 39 B3
Boscomoor Rd. ST19 39 B3
Boyden Clo. ST19 39 D3
Bramdean Dri. ST19 39 C2
Bridgewater Clo. ST19 39 C3
Brindley Clo. ST19 39 D3
Broc Clo. ST19 39 C2
Brook Clo. ST19 39 B3
Bungham La. ST19 39 A2
Cannock Rd. ST19 39 C2
Cedar Way. ST19 39 C2
Cheadle Clo. ST19 39 C3
Chelford Clo. ST19 39 C3
Chell Clo. ST19 39 C3
Cherrybrook Rd. ST19 39 C3
Chestnut Gro. ST19 39 B2
Chetwynd Clo. ST19 39 C3
Church Farm Clo. ST19 39 B2
Church Rd. ST19 39 B1
Clay St. ST19 39 B2
Commerce Dri. ST19 39 B3
Cowley Clo. ST19 39 C3
Crown Bri. ST19 39 B1
Croydon Dri. ST19 39 B2
Dene Clo. ST19 39 C2
Denefield. ST19 39 C2
Druids Way. ST19 39 C3
Edwin Clo. ST19 39 C2
Eggington Dri. ST19 39 C3
Elm Walk. ST19 39 B3
Elmdon Clo. ST19 39 C2
Fallowfield Clo. ST19 39 B2
Filance Clo. ST19 39 C3
Filance La. ST19 39 C3
Francis Clo. ST19 39 C3
Francis Green La. ST19 39 B2
Frederick Rd. ST19 39 C1
Fullmoor Clo. ST19 39 C3
Goods Station La. ST19 39 B1
Grange Clo. ST19 39 B3
Grange Cres. ST19 39 B3
Grange Rd. ST19 39 B3
Greenways. ST19 39 C2
Greville Clo. ST19 39 C3
Grocott Clo. ST19 39 B1
Grosvenor Clo. ST19 39 C1
Haling Clo. ST19 39 C2
Haling Rd. ST19 39 B1
Hatherton Rd. ST19 39 C1
Henney Clo. ST19 39 C3
Holme Rise. ST19 39 C3
Hussey Clo. ST19 39 C3
Kempson Rd. ST19 39 C3
Kentmere Clo. ST19 39 D1
Kingfisher Walk. ST19 39 C2
Knights Clo. ST19 39 C3
Leacroft Rd. ST19 39 C1
Levedale Rd. ST19 39 A1
Lime Walk. ST19 39 B3
Little Marsh Rd. ST19 39 B3
Littleton Cres. ST19 39 C1
Lock Rd. ST19 39 C3
Manorfield Clo. ST19 39 B2
Manston Hill. ST19 39 B3
Market Pl. ST19 39 B1
Market St. ST19 39 B1
Marsh La. ST19 39 C1
Mayfield Av. ST19 39 C2
Meadow Clo. ST19 39 C3
Micklewood Clo. ST19 39 C3
Mill House Gdns. ST19 39 B1
Mill St. ST19 39 B1
Moor Hall La. ST19 39 D3
Naggington Dri. ST19 39 C3
New Rd. ST19 39 B2
Newlands Clo. ST19 39 C3
Norman Rd. ST19 39 C2
Norman Rd. ST19 39 C2
Nursery Dri. ST19 39 B1
Oakley Clo. ST19 39 C3
Orchard Clo. ST19 39 C2
Orchard Cres. ST19 39 C3
Otherton Clo. ST19 39 B3
Paget Clo. ST19 39 C3
Penkridge Wharf. ST19 39 C2
Pillaton Clo. ST19 39 C2
Pinfold La. ST19 39 A2
Prescott Dri. ST19 39 B3
Preston Vale La. ST19 39 A1
Princefield Av. ST19 39 C2
Rendermore Clo. ST19 39 B3
St Michaels Clo. ST19 39 B2

St Michaels Rd. ST19 39
St Michaels Sq. ST19 39
St Modwena Way. ST19 39
Sapling Clo. ST19 39
Saxon Rd. ST19 39
Shelsey Clo. ST19 39
Sprengers Clo. ST19 39
Stamford Clo. ST19 39
Station Rd. ST19 39
Stone Cross. ST19 39
Streamside Clo. ST19 39
Teddesley Rd. ST19 39
Templars Way. ST19 39
Teveray Dri. ST19 39
The Flaxovens. ST19 39
The Saplings. ST19 39
Tildesley Clo. ST19 39
Uplands Clo. ST19 39
Vale Gdns. ST19 39
Vale Rise. ST19 39
Verdon Clo. ST19 39
Walhouse Dri. ST19 39
Waterbrook Clo. ST19 39
Wheatcroft Clo. ST19 39
Willoughby Clo. ST19 39
Wiscombe Av. ST19 39
Wolgarston Way. ST19 39
Wolverhampton Rd.
    ST19 39
Woodtherne Clo. ST19 39
Wulfric Clo. ST19 39

RUGELEY

Abbots Wk. WS15 41
Albany Dri. WS15 40
Albion St. WS15 40
Allen Birt Wk. WS15 40
Aneurin Bevan Pl. WS15 40
Anson St. WS15 40
Antler Dri. WS15 40
Arch St. WS15 40
Arden Clo. WS15 40
Armishaw Pl. WS15 40
Armitage La. WS15 40
Armitage Rd. WS15 41
Arthur Evans Clo. WS15 40
Arthur Wood Pl. WS15 40
Ashleigh Rd. WS15 40
Ashtree Bank. WS15 41
Attlee Cres. WS15 40
Averill Dri. WS15 40
Avondale Gdns. WS15 40
Bank Top. WS15 41
Barn Clo. WS15 41
Batesway. WS15 41
Bayswater Rd. WS15 40
Bedford Way. WS15 41
Beeches Rd. WS15 41
Beechmere Rise. WS15 40
Bees La. WS15 40
Bilberry Clo. WS15 40
Birch La. WS15 40
Birchtree La. WS15 41
Bishops Grange. WS15 40
Blithbury Rd. WS15 41
Bond La. WS15 40
Bow St. WS15 40
Bower La. WS15 40
Bracken Way. WS15 40
Bramble Way. WS15 40
Brereton Lodge. WS15 41
Brereton Manor Ct.
    WS15 41
Brereton Rd. WS15 40
Brewery St. WS15 40
Briar Clo. WS15 40
Brick-Kiln Way. WS15 40
Bridle Wk. WS15 41
Brindley Bank Rd. WS15 40
Brinkburn Clo. WS15 40
Brook Sq. WS15 40
*Brookside,
    Albion St. WS15 40
*Browns Way,
    Green La. WS15 40
Bryans La. WS15 40
Burnfield Dri. WS15 40
Burnthill La. WS15 41
Bush Dri. WS15 40
Byron Pl. WS15 40
Cambrian La. WS15 40
Campbell Clo. WS15 41
Canaway Wk. WS15 41
Cardigan Av. WS15 41
Catkin Wk. WS15 40
Cedar Cres. WS15 41
Chadsfield Rd. WS15 41
Chadwick. WS15 41

harnwood Clo. WS15 40 B4
hase Side Dri. WS 40 B4
haseley Clo. WS15 40 A4
herry Tree Rd. WS15 41 D7
hetwynd Clo. WS15 41 C7
heviot Dri. WS15 40 B2
hieveley Clo. WS15 40 A4
hurch Clo. WS15 40 D3
hurch Cft Gdns. WS15 40 D3
hurch La. WS15 40 A3
hurch St. WS15 40 C4
oach House La. WS15 40 C4
oalpit La. WS15 41 E8
oalway Rd. WS15 41 F7
olton Rd. WS15 40 D1
ommon La. WS15 41 B7
oppice La. WS15 41 C8
oppice La. WS15 41 C6
ornwall Ct. WS15 41 B7
oulthwaite Way. WS15 41 D6
owlishaw Way. WS15 41 E6
rabtree Way. WS15 40 A3
restwood Rise. WS15 40 A2
rocketts Nook. WS15 40 A2
ross Rd. WS15 41 C5
rossley Stone,
Sheep Fair. WS15 40 C4
urzon Pl. WS15 41 D6
affodil Wk. WS15 40 A3
avy Pl. WS15 41 C7
aywell Rise. WS15 40 B2
eacon Way. WS15 40 D3
eafield Way. WS15 40 A3
eanery Clo. WS15 40 B4
eerleap Way. WS15 40 B4
evall Clo. WS15 41 C6
evonshire Dri. WS15 41 B7
irham Rd. WS15 41 B7
xton Dri. WS15 40 A3
st Butts Rd. WS15 40 A4
dwards Dri. WS15 40 C4
lmore Ct,
Elmore La. WS15 40 D4
nore La. WS15 40 A4
sex Dri. WS15 41 B7
irmount Way. WS15 40 B4
rm Clo. WS15 40 A3
ncombe Dri. WS15 40 A3
rnwood Dri. WS15 40 B3
eld Pl. WS15 41 A5
nches Hill. WS15 40 A2
axley Rd. WS15 41 C6
rge Mews. WS15 40 D4
rge Rd. WS15 40 D4
rtescue La. WS15 40 C3
xglove Clo. WS15 40 B4
ank Gee Clo. WS15 40 C4
ank Rogers Wk.
WS15 40 B3
arden Dri. WS15 41 E6
arden Vw. WS15 40 B4
arrick Rise. WS15 41 F7
orge Brealey Clo.
WS15 41 E5
enhaven. WS15 40 B3
rse La. WS15 41 D7
rse Rd. WS15 41 D6
rseburn Way. WS15 40 A3
een La. WS15 40 B3
eenacres. WS15 41 C6
ennefields Dri. WS15 40 B4
ngley Dri. WS15 40 C4
ngley Park Gdns.
WS15 41 C5
gley Rd. WS15 40 B4
rdy Cres. WS15 41 C6
rley Clo. WS15 41 D7
rley Rd. WS15 40 D3
rney Ct. WS15 40 B2
seley Rd. WS15 40 A4
wthorne Way. WS15 41 E6
ath Rd. WS15 41 E6
ather Clo. WS15 41 D7
dnesford Rd. WS15 41 A8
ron St. WS15 40 D4
gh Falls. WS15 41 C6
gh Ridge. WS15 40 A2
ghland Way. WS15 40 A2
t St. WS15 41 C5
ary Cres. WS15 41 C7
side Clo. WS15 41 F7
ltop. WS15 41 D6
lway Clo. WS15 40 B4
lop Rd. WS15 41 C6
bbs Vw. WS15 41 F7
lly Lodge Clo. WS15 41 C5
ly Oake Pl. WS15 40 D4
rns Croft. WS15 41 A5
rse Fair. WS15 41 D5
rseshoe Dri. WS15 40 A3

Huntsmans Wk. WS15 40 B4
Hurstbourne Clo. WS15 40 A3
Hutchinson Clo. WS15 40 A3
INDUSTRIAL & RETAIL:
Lea Hall Enterprise Pk.
WS15 41 F6
Power Station Rd Ind Est.
WS15 40 D3
Redbrook La Ind Est.
WS15 41 D7
Riverside Ind Est.
WS15 40 E3
The Levels Ind Est.
WS15 41 E8
Towers Business Pk.
WS15 41 E5
Ingleside. WS15 40 B3
James Warner Clo.
WS15 40 C4
Jeffery Clo. WS15 40 B2
John Ball Ct. WS15 40 B2
John Till Clo. WS15 40 C3
Johnson Ct. WS15 40 C3
Jones La. WS15 41 A5
Joseph Dix Dri. WS15 40 C3
Jubilee St. WS15 40 B3
Kelly Av. WS15 41 D6
Kelvedon Way. WS15 40 A4
Keystone Mews. WS15 41 D5
Keystone Rd. WS15 41 D5
Kimberley Way. WS15 41 E7
King St. WS15 40 E4
Landowne Way. WS15 40 A3
Landor Cres. WS15 41 C6
Landsbury Rd. WS15 41 C6
Lanehead Wk. WS15 40 A3
Lanrick Gdns. WS15 40 D3
Larch Rd. WS15 41 E6
Lea Hall La. WS15 41 F7
Leasowe Rd. WS15 41 E7
Leathermill La. WS15 40 D4
Lees Clo. WS15 41 F7
Leyland Dri. WS15 41 D5
Lichfield St. WS15 41 D5
Lion St. WS15 40 C3
Little Orchard. WS15 40 C4
Lockside Vw. WS15 41 E5
Lodge Rd. WS15 41 F7
Love La. WS15 40 D3
Lovett Clo. WS15 40 B2
Lower Brook St. WS15 40 D4
Mckie Way. WS15 41 E6
Main Rd. WS15 41 E6
March Banks. WS15 40 B4
Marden Clo. WS15 41 D7
Market Sq. WS15 40 C4
Market St. WS15 40 C4
Mayflower Dri. WS15 40 B4
Mersey Clo. WS15 40 C2
Mill La. WS15 40 D4
Millington St. WS15 40 C4
Millside. WS15 41 A6
Moorland Clo. WS15 40 B4
Moss Grn. WS15 40 B3
Mossley. WS15 41 E5
Mount Rd. WS15 40 A3
Myatt Way. WS15 41 E6
Newman Gro. WS15 41 D6
Nursery Rd. WS15 41 E8
Oakleigh Dri. WS15 41 F7
Oakley Copse. WS15 41 A5
Oaktree Rd. WS15 41 E6
Old Chancel Rd. WS15 40 C3
Old Eaton Rd. WS15 40 C2
Orchard Clo. WS15 40 C2
Overland Clo. WS15 41 E7
Overpool Clo. WS15 40 B4
Owen Clo. WS15 41 D7
Park Hall Clo. WS15 40 C2
Park Vw Ter. WS15 40 A3
Peakes Rd. WS15 40 A3
Penk Dri North. WS15 40 A2
Penk Dri South. WS15 40 A2
Penkridge Bank Rd.
WS15 41 A5
Phoenix Clo. WS15 40 D4
Pine Vw. WS15 40 A2
Plovers Rise. WS15 40 B3
Pool Meadow Clo.
WS15 40 B4
Portobello. WS15 40 B4
Post Office La. WS15 41 A5
Power Station Rd.
WS15 40 D3
Priory Rd. WS15 41 F7
Pump La. WS15 41 C6
Pyrus Gro. WS15 41 C6
Quarry Clo. WS15 40 B2
Queen St. WS15 40 E4
Queensway. WS15 40 C3
Rangers Wk. WS15 40 A4

Ravenhill Clo. WS15 41 D6
Ravenslea Rd. WS15 41 E7
Redbrook La. WS15 41 E7
*Redmond Clo,
Dayton Dri. WS15 40 A3
Riders Way. WS15 40 A4
Rishworth Av. WS15 40 D3
Rose Way. WS15 40 B2
Rowley Clo. WS15 41 E7
Rutherglen Clo. WS15 40 A3
Rutland Av. WS15 41 B7
St Anthonys Clo. WS15 40 D4
St Augustines Rd.
WS15 41 C7
St Edwards Grn. WS15 41 C6
St Johns Clo. WS15 41 A5
St Michaels Dri. WS15 41 E7
St Michaels Dri. WS15 41 E7
St Pauls Rd. WS15 41 D5
Sandy La. WS15 41 C6
Sankey Cres. WS15 41 C6
Sarah Challinor Clo.
WS15 41 C5
*Scholars Gate,
Seabrook Rd. WS15 41 F7
School Rd. WS15 40 B3
Seabrook Rd. WS15 41 F7
Setterfield Way. WS15 41 D6
Shaftsbury Rd. WS15 41 C6
Sharnbrook Rd. WS15 40 B3
Sheep Fair. WS15 40 C4
Sheringham Dri. WS15 40 A3
Shrewsbury Mall. WS15 40 D4
Shugborough Rd. WS15 40 B2
Slitting Mill Rd. WS15 41 A6
Somerset Av. WS15 41 C7
Speechly Dri. WS15 40 C3
Springfields Rd. WS15 40 B2
Springhill Av. WS15 41 E6
Springhill Ter. WS15 41 D6
Spruce Wk. WS15 40 A2
Stag Clo. WS15 40 A3
Station Rd. WS15 40 D3
Stile Clo. WS15 41 D7
Stile Cop Rd. WS15 41 B7
Surrey Clo. WS15 41 B7
Sutton Clo. WS15 41 D6
Swallow Clo. WS15 40 C3
Swan Clo. WS15 41 F8
Sycamore Cres. WS15 41 F7
Talbot Rd. WS15 41 D5
Talbot St. WS15 41 D5
Tannery Clo. WS15 40 E4
Taylors La. WS15 40 D4
The Beeches. WS15 40 B2
The Green. WS15 41 E7
The Laurels. WS15 41 D6
The Oaklands. WS15 40 A4
The Rise. WS15 41 E7
The Slade. WS15 41 E8
The Stables. WS15 40 C4
The Willows. WS15 41 F8
Thistle Clo. WS15 40 A3
Thompson Rd. WS15 41 F7
Thorn Clo. WS15 41 E6
Tithebarn Rd. WS15 40 C3
Toy Clo. WS15 40 B3
Trentview Clo. WS15 41 E6
Tunnicliffe Dri. WS15 40 C3
Upfield Way. WS15 40 B3
Uplands Gdns. WS15 41 C7
Upper Brook St. WS15 40 D4
Upper Cross Rd. WS15 41 C5
Upton Pl. WS15 40 C3
Vicars Croft. WS15 40 D3
Walnut La. WS15 41 F7
Wat Tyler Clo. WS15 40 C2
Waterside. WS15 41 E7
Watfield Clo. WS15 41 F8
Watkiss Dri. WS15 40 A3
Watson Clo. WS15 40 C2
Waverley Gdns. WS15 40 A3
Weatherall Clo. WS15 40 B3
Wellington Dri. WS15 40 D4
Western Springs Rd.
WS15 40 C2
Western View. WS15 40 C2
Wharf Rd. WS15 41 D5
Whitgreave La. WS15 40 A3
Whitworth La. WS15 40 A3
William Morris Ct. WS15 40 B2
Winstanley Clo. WS15 40 B3
Winstanley Pl. WS15 40 C2
Wolseley Rd. WS15 40 A1
Woodcock Rd. WS15 40 A4
Woodhayes Lawns.
WS15 40 A4
Woodthorne Clo. WS15 40 B3
Woodview. WS15 41 E7
Yew Tree Rd. WS15 41 E6

STAFFORD

Abbots Walk. ST16 43 E5
Albert Ter. ST16 43 E5
Aldbury Clo. ST16 43 E1
Alder Gro. ST17 44 C4
Aldershaw Clo. ST16 42 D1
Aldrin Clo. ST16 43 H5
Alexandra Rd. ST17 45 F2
Allendale. ST16 42 C2
Alliance St. ST16 42 D4
Allotment La. ST16 44 D2
Alstone Clo. ST16 42 B3
Amblefield Way. ST16 42 D1
Ampleforth Dri. ST17 45 H3
Ardingley Av. ST17 45 H3
Armstrong Av. ST16 43 H5
Ashdale Dri. ST16 42 D1
Ashley Clo. ST16 42 B5
Ashridge Walk. ST16 43 E1
Aspen Croft. ST17 44 C4
Aston Ter. ST16 43 E3
Astonfields Rd. ST16 43 E4
Astoria St. ST17 45 F5
Attlee Cres. ST17 44 D4
Auden Way. ST17 44 C3
Austin Friars. ST17 45 E2
Averil Rd. ST17 44 D4
Avon Rise. ST16 43 H6
Back Browning St. ST16 43 E5
Bagots Oak. ST17 44 C4
Barker Clo. ST16 44 C1
Barlaston Clo. ST16 42 D1
Barley St. ST16 42 B5
Barn Bank La. ST17 44 D6
Barns Rd. ST17 44 D5
Batholdi Way. ST17 45 G3
Baxter Grn. ST16 42 C6
Beaconside. ST16 42 D1
Beaconside Clo. ST16 43 G4
Beaumont Gdns. ST17 44 C3
Bedford Av. ST16 43 G6
Beechcroft Av. ST17 44 D2
Beechway. ST16 42 D3
Beeston Ridge. ST17 44 C4
Belfort Way. ST17 45 G4
Bell Clo. ST16 43 F5
Bellasis St. ST16 43 E4
Benenden Clo. ST17 45 H3
Berry Rd. ST16 42 B2
Bertelin Rd. ST16 43 G3
Betjeman Way. ST17 44 C5
Beton Way. ST16 42 D4
Betty Hatch La. ST16 42 C1
Beverley Dri. ST16 42 C2
Bigwood La. ST16 44 A6
Billington Bank. ST18 44 A4
Binyon Ct. ST17 44 C4
Birch Gro. ST17 44 C4
Blackberry La. ST16 42 D6
Blakiston St. ST16 43 G5
Blythe Rd. ST17 45 F6
Boardman Cres. ST16 44 D1
Boningale Way. ST17 44 B3
Bonington Cres. ST16 44 B3
Boon Gro. ST17 45 F6
Border Way. ST17 45 F5
Bracken Clo. ST17 44 A6
Brackenfield Way. ST16 42 D1
Bradbury Rise. ST16 42 B5
Bradshaw Way. ST16 43 E1
Bramall La. ST16 42 C3
Bridge St. ST16 45 E1
Brindley Clo. ST16 43 F1
Brisbane St. ST17 44 C3
Broad Eye. ST16 43 E6
Broad Meadow Croft.
ST16 42 B5
Broad St. ST16 43 E6
Bromstead Cres. ST16 42 B3
Brook Ct. ST17 44 C4
Brook Glen Clo. ST17 45 E4
Brook Glen Rd. ST17 45 E4
Brooklime Gdns. ST16 42 B5
Broughton Clo. ST16 42 D2
Browning St. ST16 43 E5
Brundle Av. ST16 44 C1
Brunel Clo. ST16 43 F1
Brunswick Ter. ST17 45 E2
Buckland Rd. ST16 42 D1
Burcham Clo. ST16 42 C3
Burlington Dri. ST17 44 B5
Burnett Ct. ST16 43 E5
Burns Av. ST17 44 D5
Bursley Clo. ST17 44 D6
Burton Bank La. ST16 44 D6
Burton Manor Rd. ST17 45 E5
Burton Sq. ST17 45 E5
Busbys Bldg. ST16 43 E5

Byron Clo. ST16 43 G5
Cairns Dri. ST16 43 H5
Cambridge St. ST16 43 G6
Cameo Way. ST16 42 B2
Cape Av. ST17 44 C4
Carder Av. ST16 42 C2
Carisbrooke Dri. ST17 44 B4
Carling Clo. ST16 44 C1
Carlton Sq. ST17 44 B3
Carson Way. ST16 44 C1
Carver Rd. ST16 43 F3
Castle Acre. ST17 44 A3
Castle Bank. ST17 44 A3
Castle St. ST16 42 D6
Castle Way. ST16 44 D2
Castledene Dri. ST16 44 C2
Castlefields. ST16 44 D1
Catalan Clo. ST17 45 G4
Caulden Rd. ST16 42 D1
Charles Cotton St. ST16 42 D1
Charnley Rd. ST16 43 F4
Charterhouse Av. ST17 45 H3
Chartley Clo. ST16 42 D1
Chaucer Rd. ST17 44 C3
Chebsey Rd. ST16 42 B3
Chell Rd. ST16 44 A6
Chelsea Way. ST17 44 D2
Chesham Rd. ST16 43 G4
Chetney Clo. ST16 42 C5
Christie Av. ST16 44 C1
Christopher Ter. ST17 45 G2
Church Clo. ST17 45 F6
Churchill Way. ST17 45 E6
Clanford Clo. ST17 45 F6
Clare Rd. ST16 42 D3
Claremont Gro. ST16 44 B3
Clarendon Dri. ST17 44 B3
Clement Clo. ST16 43 G5
Cleveland Walk. ST17 44 B3
Clifton Clo. ST16 43 H6
Clifton Dri. ST16 43 H6
Co-operative St. ST16 43 E4
Coghlan Dri. ST17 44 D4
Cole Dri. ST16 44 C1
Coleridge Dri. ST17 44 C4
Common Rd. ST16 43 E1
Common Walk. ST16 43 E4
Commonside Clo. ST16 43 E4
Compton Clo. ST17 45 G2
Conway Rd. ST16 42 B5
Cope St. ST16 45 F1
Copper Glade. ST16 43 H6
Coronation Rd. ST16 43 G4
Corporation St. ST16 43 E5
Coton Av. ST16 43 H6
County Rd. ST16 43 E5
Coventry Ct. ST16 42 B5
Cowan Dri. ST16 43 G6
Cowley Clo. ST17 44 C3
Crab La. ST16 42 B2
Crabbery St. ST16 43 E6
Craddock Rd. ST16 42 C3
Cramer St. ST17 45 F2
Cranberry Clo. ST16 42 B3
Cranbrook Walk. ST17 44 B3
Crescent Rd. ST17 45 E2
Creswell Ct. ST16 42 A2
Creswell St. ST18 42 A2
Creswell Farm Dri. ST16 42 B3
Creswell Rd. ST18 42 A1
Crinan Gro. ST17 44 D5
Crispin Clo. ST16 42 D2
Crooked Bridge Rd.
ST16 43 E5
Cross St. ST16 43 E5
Crossway. ST16 45 G1
Cull Av. ST16 43 H6
Daimler Clo. ST17 45 H3
Danby Crest. ST17 44 B3
Darnford Clo. ST16 42 D1
Dart Av. ST17 44 B4
Dartmouth St. ST16 45 G1
Daurada Dri. ST17 45 G4
Davies Clo. ST16 43 G6
Deanshill Clo. ST16 44 D2
Dearnsdale Clo. ST16 42 B2
Delamere La. ST17 44 B4
Dell Clo. ST16 42 C2
Denstone Av. ST17 45 H3
Denver Fold. ST17 44 B3
Denzil Grn. ST17 44 B3
Derby St. ST16 45 E1
Devon Way. ST17 44 B4
Dexter Rise. ST17 44 B4
Dickson Rd. ST16 43 G5
Dorrington Dri. ST16 43 E4
Douglas Rd. ST16 43 G5
Douglas Rd West. ST16 43 G5
Dove Clo. ST17 45 F6
Downderrry Clo. ST17 44 B4

Downfield Gro. ST16 42 D1
Doxey. ST16 42 A6
Doxey Fields. ST16 42 A5
Doxey Rd. ST16 42 D6
Dreieich Clo. ST16 43 F5
Drummond Rd. ST16 43 E4
Dryburgh Clo. ST17 44 C5
Dryden Cres. ST17 44 C3
Dunster Clo. ST17 44 B4
Earl St. ST16 45 E1
Easby Clo. ST17 44 C4
Eastgate St. ST16 43 E6
Eastlands. ST17 45 E3
Eastlands Clo. ST17 45 E3
Eastlands Gro. ST17 45 F3
Eccleshall Rd. ST16 42 B2
Edison Rd. ST16 43 F4
Edmund Av. ST17 44 C3
Edwards Dri. ST16 44 C1
Edwin Clo. ST17 44 C3
Elford Clo. ST16 42 D1
Eliot Way. ST17 44 C3
Ellington Av. ST16 43 H5
Elmhurst Clo. ST16 42 D1
Elsdon Rd. ST17 44 D5
Elworthy Clo. ST16 43 G4
Embry Av. ST16 43 G5
Espleys Yd. ST16 45 E1
Eton Clo. ST17 45 H3
Exeter St. ST17 45 F3
Fairfield Ct. ST17 43 F4
Fairoak Av. ST16 42 D2
Fairway. ST16 45 G1
Fancy Walk. ST16 43 E5
Faraday Rd. ST16 43 F5
Felden Clo. ST16 43 E1
Fellfield Way. ST16 43 E1
Fern Dri. ST16 42 B5
Fernleigh Gdns. ST16 42 A5
Fernwood. ST16 42 D2
Field Pl. ST16 43 E3
First Av. ST16 42 C2
Fonthil Rd. ST16 43 F3
Foregate St. ST16 43 E5
Frank Foley Way. ST16 42 D5
Freemen St. ST16 43 F4
Frew Clo. ST16 43 H6
Friar St. ST16 45 E1
Friars Rd. ST16 45 E1
Friars Ter. ST17 45 E2
Frinton Clo. ST16 43 G3
Furness Gro. ST17 44 C5
Gaol Rd. ST16 43 E5
Gaolgate St. ST16 43 E6
Garden Pl. ST17 45 F2
Garden St. ST17 45 F2
Garrod Sq. ST16 43 H5
Garth Clo. ST17 45 F6
George Bailey Ct. ST17 45 F3
George St. ST16 43 E5
Gibson Clo. ST16 43 F4
Gillingham Cres. ST16 44 C1
Glebe Av. ST16 42 D3
Glebelands. ST17 45 F6
Globe Av. ST17 45 F5
Glover St. ST16 43 E6
Gordon Av. ST16 42 D2
Gorsebrook Leys. ST16 42 A4
Gough Clo. ST17 44 C2
Grassmere Hollow. ST16 42 A5
Gray Walk. ST17 44 C4
Greengate St. ST16 45 E1
Greensome Clo. ST16 42 B5
Greensome Ct. ST16 42 B5
Greensome Cres. ST16 42 A5
Greensome La. ST16 42 A5
Greenway. ST16 45 G1
Greenways. ST18 44 C6
Greenwood Gro. ST17 44 D4
Greyfriars. ST16 43 E5
Greyfriars Pl. ST16 43 E5
Greyfriars Way. ST16 42 D5
Grissom Clo. ST16 43 H5
Gunnel Clo. ST16 44 C1
Hall Clo. ST17 45 G4
Hambridge Clo. ST17 44 D5
Harcourt Way. ST16 42 C2
Hardy Rd. ST17 44 C3
Hargreaves La. ST17 44 D2
Harmony Grn. ST17 44 C4
Harris Rd. ST16 43 H5
Harrowby St. ST16 45 H1
Hartwell Gro. ST17 42 B3
Hatherton St. ST16 45 G1
Hawke Rd. ST16 42 C3
Hawksmoor Rd. ST17 44 B4
Hawthorn Av. ST17 45 G2
Hazel Gro. ST16 42 C2
Hazleton Grn. ST17 45 E5
Hearn Ct. ST17 45 E5

Heath Dri. ST16 42 C2
Heenan Gro. ST17 45 F6
Helen Sharman Dri. ST16 43 H5
Helford Gro. ST17 44 C4
Henry St. ST16 43 F4
Herbert Rd. ST17 45 E3
Hesketh Rd. ST17 45 E5
High Park. ST16 44 C2
Highfield Gro. ST17 44 D4
Highlands. ST17 44 D4
Hill Crest. ST17 44 D4
Hillcote Hollow. ST16 42 B3
Hillfarm Clo. ST17 45 F6
Hinton Clo. ST17 45 G6
Holbeach Way. ST16 42 B5
Holmcroft Rd. ST16 42 C3
Holmes Clo. ST16 44 C1
Homestead Ct. ST16 43 E2
Hopton Clo. ST16 43 E4
Hopton La. ST16 43 H1
Hopton St. ST16 43 F4
Howard Rd. ST17 45 F5
Hurlingham Rd. ST16 42 C2
Hyde Ct. ST17 45 E4
Hyde Lea Bank. ST18 44 D6
INDUSTRIAL & RETAIL:
Astonfields Ind Est. ST16 43 F3
Astonfields Rd Business Pk. ST16 43 F4
Carver Rd Business Pk. ST16 43 F3
Common Rd Ind Est. ST16 43 F2
Dorrington Ind Pk. ST16 43 E4
Greyfriars Business Pk. ST16 42 D5
Palmbourne Ind Pk. ST16 44 D1
Queens Retail Pk. ST17 45 G3
St Albans Rd Ind Est. ST16 43 F1
Tollgate Ind Pk. ST16 43 F1
Ingestre Rd. ST17 45 F2
Inglewood. ST17 44 D2
Isabel Clo. ST17 44 C3
Izaak Walton Clo. ST16 42 D4
Izaak Walton St. ST16 42 D4
Jacobs Croft. ST16 42 D2
Jerningham St. ST16 42 D6
John Amery Dri. ST17 45 E5
John Donne St. ST16 42 D3
John St. ST16 43 G6
Jones Clo. ST17 44 D4
Jubilee Ct. ST16 43 F5
Jupiter Way. ST17 45 G4
Keats Av. ST17 44 C4
Keld Av. ST17 44 B4
Kendal Clo. ST17 44 B4
Kennedy Way. ST16 44 C2
Kent Way. ST17 45 H4
Kentish Clo. ST17 44 B4
Kentmere Clo. ST17 44 B4
Kenworthy Rd. ST16 43 E3
Keswick Gro. ST17 44 A4
Kimberley Way. ST17 44 B4
Kingsley Clo. ST17 45 E4
Kingsley Rd. ST17 45 E4
Kingston Av. ST16 43 H6
Kingsway. ST16 44 D1
Kirkstall Av. ST17 44 C4
Knight Av. ST16 43 G5
Lammascote Rd. ST16 45 F1
Lancaster Rd. ST17 44 A5
Lancing Av. ST17 45 H3
landstone Rd. ST17 44 C6
Lansbury Clo. ST17 45 E3
Lapley Av. ST16 42 B3
Lara Clo. ST16 44 C1
Larkin Clo. ST17 44 C5
Laurel Gro. ST17 45 F4
Lawn Rd. ST17 44 D3
Lawnsfield Walk. ST16 42 D1
Lawrence St. ST17 45 F3
Lea Cres. ST16 45 E4
Lea Gro. ST16 42 D2
Leigh Clo. ST17 45 F6
Lethbridge Gdns. ST17 44 B4
Levedale Clo. ST16 42 B3
Lexington Grn. ST17 44 B4
Liberty Park. ST17 44 B3
Lichfield Rd. ST17 45 F2
Lilac Gro. ST17 45 F5
Lilleshall Way. ST17 44 C4
Limetree Av. ST16 43 E4
Lincoln Meadows. ST17 44 D2
Lindon Clo. ST17 44 C4
Lineker Clo. ST17 44 C1

Linksfield Gro. ST16 42 D1
Lion Way. ST17 45 G4
Lister Rd. ST16 43 F5
Lloyd St. ST16 43 E5
Longshore Clo. ST16 44 D5
Lotus Way. ST16 43 F4
Lovatt St. ST16 43 E4
Lovelace Clo. ST17 44 D3
Loynton Clo. ST16 42 B3
Lyric Clo. ST17 45 F5
Lyttleton Ct. ST16 43 G6
Malcolm Rd. ST17 45 E6
Mallard Av. ST17 45 H4
Malvern Clo. ST17 45 H3
Manor Farm Cres. ST17 45 E6
Manor Grn. ST17 44 D5
Manor Sq. ST17 45 E5
Mansel Clo. ST16 44 D1
Maple Gro. ST17 45 F4
Market Sq. ST16 43 E6
Market St. ST16 43 E6
Marlowe Rd. ST17 44 C3
Marsh Ct. ST16 43 E4
Marsh St. ST16 43 E5
Marsland Clo. ST16 42 B5
Marsland Rd. ST16 42 B5
Marston Ct. ST16 43 E4
Marston Dri. ST16 43 E4
Marston Ho. ST16 43 E4
Marston Rd. ST16 43 E5
Marsworth Way. ST16 42 D1
Martin Av. ST16 44 C1
Martin St. ST16 43 E6
Mary Rand Clo. ST17 45 E4
Masefield Dri. ST17 44 C3
Matthews Rd. ST17 44 D5
Mayock Cres. ST16 44 C1
Meadow St. ST17 45 G4
Meadow Rd. ST17 45 G4
Meadowbank Wk. ST16 42 D1
Meakin Gro. ST16 42 C3
Melbourne Cres. ST16 43 H5
Melrose Av. ST17 45 C4
Merrey Rd. ST17 45 E5
Merrivale Rd. ST17 45 F4
Meyrick Rd. ST17 45 F2
Mill Bank. ST16 45 E1
Mill St. ST16 45 E1
Milton Gro. ST17 44 C4
Moorfields. ST16 42 D3
Morton Rd. ST17 45 E5
Mosspit. ST17 45 F6
Mossvale Gro. ST16 42 A5
Mount Edge. ST16 43 H1
Mount St. ST16 43 G6
Mountville Dri. ST17 44 C3
Mynors St. ST16 43 G6
Nash Av. ST16 42 C3
Nelson Way. ST17 45 E6
New Garden St. ST17 45 F2
New St. ST16 43 E5
Newall Av. ST16 43 H5
Newland Av. ST16 42 D2
Newport Rd. ST17 44 B3
Newton Rd. ST16 43 G4
Norfolk Way. ST17 44 D5
North Av. ST16 42 D3
North Castle St. ST16 42 D6
North Pl. ST16 43 E4
North Walls. ST16 43 E6
Nursery La. ST16 42 D5
Oak Tree Clo. ST17 44 B4
Oaklands Dri. ST17 44 D2
Orchard St. ST17 45 F2
Orwell Dri. ST16 44 B4
Oulton Way. ST16 42 B3
Owen Walk. ST17 44 C5
Oxford Gdns. ST16 43 F4
Oxleathers Ct. ST17 44 C4
Paddock Clo. ST16 42 C2
Pantulf Clo. ST17 45 G3
Park Av. ST17 45 E4
Park Cres. ST17 45 E3
Park St. ST17 45 E4
Parkers Croft Rd. ST17 45 F2
Parkfields. ST17 44 D4
Parkside Av. ST16 42 D1
Peach Av. ST17 45 F5
Peel St. ST16 43 E6
Peel Ter. ST16 43 E4
Penkvale Rd. ST16 44 B4
Pennycroft Bungalows. ST16 44 B4
Perrin Clo. ST17 45 F5
Peter James Ct. ST16 43 F4
Pike Clo. ST16 43 H4
Pintail Clo. ST17 45 H5
Pitstone Clo. ST16 43 E1
Pitt St. ST16 42 D6
Plant Av. ST17 45 F5
Pope Gdns. ST17 44 C5

Poplar Way. ST17 45 E6
Portal Rd. ST16 43 H4
Prescott Av. ST16 43 G5
Prestwood Ct. ST17 45 F2
Princes St. ST16 43 E6
Princess Pl. ST16 43 E4
Prospect Rd. ST16 43 F5
Pulteney Dri. ST16 42 C3
Queensville. ST17 45 H3
Queensville Av. ST17 45 G2
Queensville Bri. ST17 45 G2
Queensway. ST16 43 E6
Radford Bank. ST17 45 H4
Railway St. ST16 44 D1
Ralph Ct. ST17 44 D3
Rambleford Way. ST16 42 D1
Read Av. ST16 43 G5
Reason Rd. ST17 45 F6
Red Lion St. ST16 43 E6
Redgrave Dri. ST16 44 C1
Redhill. ST16 42 C2
Redhill Gorse. ST16 42 C1
Repton Clo. ST17 45 H3
Reva Rd. ST17 45 F4
Rhein Way. ST17 45 G3
Richards Av. ST16 43 G6
Richmond Clo. ST17 45 E4
Rickerscote Av. ST17 45 G5
Rickerscote Hall La. ST17 45 G6
Rickerscote Rd. ST17 45 F6
Rising Brook. ST17 45 E4
Riversmeade Way. ST16 42 A5
Riverway. ST16 45 G2
Roedean Av. ST17 45 H3
Romford Rd. ST16 43 F3
Romney Dri. ST16 42 B5
Rose Hill. ST16 44 C1
Rotherwood Dri. ST17 44 D3
Rouse Clo. ST16 44 C1
Rowley Av. ST17 44 D3
Rowley Bank. ST17 45 E3
Rowley Bank Gdns. ST17 45 E3
Rowley Gro. ST17 45 E3
Rowley Hall Clo. ST17 44 D3
Rowley Hall Dri. ST17 44 D3
Rowley St. ST16 45 E3
Rye Ct. ST16 42 A5
Sabine St. ST17 45 F3
St Albans Rd. ST16 43 E3
St Andrews Rd. ST17 44 D4
St Davids Rd. ST17 44 D4
St Georges Rd. ST17 45 G2
St Johns Rd. ST17 45 F3
St Johns Walk. ST16 43 G6
St Leonards Av. ST17 45 G2
St Patricks St. ST17 45 E3
St Peters Clo. ST17 45 F6
St Peters Gdns. ST17 45 F6
St Thomas St. ST16 43 G6
Salisbury Dri. ST16 43 H5
Salisbury Rd. ST16 43 H5
Salmond Av. ST16 43 H5
Salt Av. ST17 45 F2
Salt Rd. ST17 45 F2
Salter St. ST16 43 E6
Sandalwood Dri. ST16 43 F4
Sandon Mews. ST16 43 F4
Sandon Rd. ST16 43 E5
Sandown Croft. ST17 44 D2
Sandyford St. ST16 43 H5
Sash St. ST16 43 E6
Savourese Dri. ST17 45 G4
Sayers Rd. ST16 42 B3
School La. ST17 45 F6
School Lane Clo. ST17 45 F6
School Pl. ST16 43 F5
Searle Av. ST16 44 C1
Second Av. ST16 42 C2
Shakespeare Rd. ST17 44 C3
Shallowford Mews. ST16 42 D4
Shannon Rd. ST17 44 D5
Shaw Gdns. ST17 44 C3
Shebdon Clo. ST16 42 B3
Shelley Clo. ST16 43 G5
Shelmore Clo. ST16 42 C2
Shenley Gro. ST17 44 D5
Sheridan St. ST16 43 H4
Sherwood Av. ST17 45 E4
Shrewsbury Rd. ST17 45 F2
Sidney Av. ST17 45 F5
Siemens Rd. ST17 45 F4
Silkmore Cres. ST17 45 G4
Silkmore La. ST17 45 G5
Simpson Clo. ST16 42 C3
Slessor Rd. ST16 43 G5
Smallman St. ST16 43 G5
Snows Yd. ST16 43 E5

Somerset Rd. ST17 44
Somerville Sq. ST17 45
South St. ST16 45
South Walls. ST16 45
Southfields Clo. ST16 45
Southfields Rd. ST17 45
Speedwell Rise. ST16 42
Spencer Clo. ST17 44
Spode Av. ST16 43
Springfield Dri. ST17 45
Springvale Rise. ST16 42
Stafford St. ST16 43
Stanway Ct. ST16 43
Station Rd. ST16 44
Steadman Cres. ST17 45
Stevenson Dri. ST17 44
Stone Rd. ST16 43
Stone Rd. ST16 43
Stretton Av. ST16 43
Stychfields. ST17 45
Sundown Dri. ST17 44
Surrey Rd. ST17 44
Sutton Dri. ST16 42
Swan Clo. ST16 43
Swinburne Clo. ST17 44
Sycamore La. ST17 45
Talbot Rd. ST17 44
Tamar Gro. ST17 45
Taplin Clo. ST16 42
Tarragonia Dri. ST17 45
Taylor Walk. ST17 44
Tedder Rd. ST16 45
Telegraph St. ST17 45
Telford Dri. ST16 43
Tenby Dri. ST16 44
Tennyson Rd. ST17 44
Tenterbanks. ST16 45
Thackery Walk. ST17 44
Thames Way. ST17 44
The Birches. ST17 45
The Brandons. ST17 44
The Close. ST16 45
The Close. ST17 45
The Crescent. ST16 42
The Drive. ST16 42
The Glade. ST17 45
The Green. ST17 45
The Haybarn. ST16 43
The Lawn. ST17 45
The Oval. ST16 45
The Ridgeway. ST16 42
The Rockeries. ST17 45
The Russetts. ST17 44
Thirlmere Way. ST17 45
Thomas Av. ST16 44
Thompson Clo. ST17 44
Thornyfields La. ST16 44
Tillington St. ST16 43
Tipping St. ST16 45
Tithe Barn Clo. ST17 43
Tithe Barn Rd. ST16 43
Tixall Rd. ST16 43
Tollgate Dri. ST17 43
Torridge Dri. ST17 44
Trenchard Av. ST16 44
Trent Clo. ST17 45
Trevelyans Grn. ST16 44
Trinity Gorse. ST16 42
Trinity Rise. ST16 42
Tudor Rise. ST16 42
Tudor Way. ST17 42
Tullis Clo. ST16 44
Turney Gro. ST17 44
Turnhill Clo. ST17 44
Tyra Way. ST17 45
Underwood Clo. ST16 42
Uplands Rd. ST16 43
Upmeadows Dri. ST16 44
Vaughan Way. ST17 44
Verulam Ct. ST16 43
Verulam Rd. ST17 43
Vicarage Way. ST17 44
Victoria Rd. ST16 44
Victoria Sq. ST16 43
Victoria St. ST16 43
Victoria Ter. ST16 44
Virginia Av. ST17 45
Walden Av. ST16 45
Walland Gro. ST16 45
Warrens La. ST16 44
Warwick Rd. ST17 45
Washington Dri. ST17 45
Water St. ST16 45
Wayfield Dri. ST16 45
Weaver Dri. ST17 44
Wellington Clo. ST16 45
West Clo. ST16 45
West Way. ST17 45
West Way Grn. ST17 44
Westbury Hayes. ST17 44
Westhead Av. ST16 45

STOKE-UPON-TRENT

INDUSTRIAL & RETAIL:

STONE

TAMWORTH

eltic. B77 52 D4
ennis. B77 52 C3
ent St. B79 51 F4
erwent. B77 52 B4
evereux Ho. B79 50 D4
orado. B77 53 B7
ormer Av. B77 51 G4
osthill Rd. B77 53 B6
owning Dri. B79 50 B4
aycott Cres. B77 52 A4
yden Rd. B79 50 D2
umolos La. B77 52 C2
unedin. B77 52 E4
unstall La. B78 50 A4
unster. B77 53 A6
gle Dri. B77 52 F2
lingham. B77 52 F4
st St. B77 53 B8
st Vw. B77 52 C2
ale. B77 52 F4
gar Clo. B79 50 C2
ithas Clo. B79 51 E4
wart Ct. B77 51 H5
ward St. B79 50 D4
zabeth Dri. B79 50 D3
erbeck. B77 52 F4
nhurst Dri. B78 50 D6
gine La. B77 52 E3
ingden. B77 52 F4
chell Rd. B78 50 C6
helfleda Rd. B77 53 D8
eter Dri. B79 50 B3
ley. B77 52 B4
irview Clo. B77 52 D1
irway. B77 53 C8
lcon. B77 53 E7
lna Cres. B79 50 C2
ringdon. B77 52 D4
rm CLo. B79 51 F2
zeley Rd. B78 50 D5
zeley Rd. B78 51 E6
lspar Rd. B77 52 E3
nn St. B77 53 B5
rrers Rd. B77 52 B1
ld Farm La. B77 52 B4
tree Clo. B79 50 B1
ra Clo. B79 51 F2
rendine St. B77 52 D1
ntenaye Rd. B79 50 B1
rties. B77 53 B6
ssdale Rd. B77 53 E5
xglove. B77 52 E2
asley La. B77 53 E7
ville Clo. B79 50 D3
rness. B77 52 B3
garin. B79 50 C4
lena Clo. B77 52 F3
lliers Clo. B77 53 D8
rrigill. B77 53 E5
tcombe Pl. B79 51 E2
wsnorth. B79 50 A2
yle. B77 52 E4
orge St. B79 51 E5
rard. B79 50 B2
lway La. B79 50 D1
ascote Clo. B77 51 G5
lascote La. B77 53 D6
Glascote Rd. B77 52 A2
Glendale Ct. B77 53 F7
Gleneagles. B77 52 F1
Glyndebourne. B79 50 A2
Godolphin. B79 50 A2
Gofton. B77 53 E5
Goldcrest. B77 53 E8
Goldsborough. B77 53 E5
Goldsmith Pl. B79 50 D2
Goostry Clo. B77 51 G4
Goostry Rd. B77 51 G4
Gorsy Bank Rd. B77 53 D8
Grange Clo. B77 53 A5
Granville. B77 52 D5
Grassholme. B77 53 E5
Grayling. B77 53 B7
Grayston Av. B77 52 C2
Great Mead. B77 52 A4
Greenhart. B77 52 E2
Greenhill Clo. B77 53 A8
Greenlea. B77 53 E5
Gresley. B77 52 D4
Grindsbrook. B77 53 E5
Gurnard. B77 53 B7
Guys Clo. B79 50 C2
Hadrians Clo. B77 53 A5
Halford St. B79 50 D4
Haltonlea. B77 53 E5
Hamble. B77 52 B3
Hampton Clo. B79 51 F2
Hanbury Rd. B77 52 D1
Hanlith. B77 53 E5
Harcourt Ho. B79 50 D5
© Harebell. B77 52 E1

Hartleyburn. B77 53 E5
Harwell Clo. B79 51 F2
Hastings Clo. B77 53 D7
Hawfinch. B77 53 D8
Hawkside. B77 53 E5
Hawksworth. B77 52 D4
Hawthorne Av. B79 50 D1
Hayle. B77 52 B4
Hayworth Clo. B79 50 C1
Hazel Garth. B77 53 E5
Heath St. B79 51 F4
Hebden. B77 53 F5
Hedging La. B77 53 B8
Helmingham. B79 50 A2
Helston Clo. B79 51 F1
Henley Clo. B79 51 F3
Hesleden. B77 53 E5
High St. B77 53 A8
Highcliffe Rd. B77 53 B5
Highfield Av. B77 52 D1
Highgrove Clo. B79 51 E2
Hillcrest Clo. B79 51 E3
Hillman. B77 52 C3
Hilltop Av. B79 51 E1
Hilmore Way. B77 53 C6
Hockley Rd. B77 53 C8
Hodge La. B77 52 F1
Holly Clo. B79 51 E2
Holsworth Clo. B77 52 B4
Holwick. B77 53 F5
Honeybourne. B77 52 B3
Hopleys Clo. B77 52 C2
Hornbeam. B77 52 E1
Hospital St. B79 51 E4
Houting. B77 53 B8
Hoylake. B77 52 F1
INDUSTRIAL & RETAIL:
Amber Business Village. B77 52 F2
Amington Ind Est. B77 52 F3
Beauchamp Ind Pk. B77 53 B5
Cardinal Point Distribution Pk. B78 50 C6
Castle Trading Est. B79 50 B3
Cedar Pk. B77 53 B8
Centurian Pk Ind Est. B77 53 F7
Hedging La Ind Est. B77 53 C8
Lichfield Ind Est. B79 50 B3
Lichfield Rd Ind Est. B79 50 C4
Ninian Pk. B77 53 B7
Pebble Close Business Village. B77 52 F2
Tame Valley Ind Est. B77 53 C7
Tame Valle Ind Est. B77 53 C6
Tame Valley Business Centre. B77 53 C7
Two Gates Ind Est. B77 53 B6
Ventura Retail Pk. B78 50 D6
Ventura Shopping Centre. B78 50 D6
Viking Pk. B77 53 B6
Ingram Pit La. B77 52 E1
Iris Clo. B79 51 F3
Irwell. B77 52 C4
Ivatt. B77 52 D3
Ivyhouse Wk. B77 53 D7
Jaguar. B77 52 C3
Jasmine Rd. B77 52 E1
Jason Clo. B77 51 G4
Jenson. B77 52 C3
Jervis Rd. B77 53 D8
Jessop Dri. B77 51 G4
John Dory. B77 53 B7
John St. B77 52 B2
Johns St. B79 51 E4
Jonkel Av. B77 53 D8
Jowett. B77 52 B3
June Cres. B77 51 H4
Juniper. B77 52 E1
Keats Clo. B79 50 C1
Kenilworth Rd. B77 52 C1
Kennedy Clo. B77 53 A5
Kennet. B77 52 B4
Kensington Dri. B77 51 E2
Kentwell. B79 50 A2
Kepler. B79 50 B2
Kerria Rd. B77 52 E1
Kestrel. B77 53 E7
Kettlebrook Rd. B77 52 A2
Kilbye Clo. B77 53 D8
Kimberley. B77 53 D6

King St. B79 51 E4
Kingfisher. B77 53 E7
Kingsley Clo. B79 50 D3
Kingston Clo. B79 51 F2
Kipling Rise. B79 50 C1
Kirtley. B77 52 C4
Kurtus. B77 53 B7
Laburnum Av. B79 51 E1
Lady Bank. B79 51 E5
Lagonda. B77 52 B3
Lagrange. B79 50 B3
Lakeland Dri. B77 53 E6
Lakenheath. B79 51 F2
Lamprey. B77 53 B7
Lanchester Clo. B79 50 C2
Landsberg. B79 50 C3
Lansdowne Cres. B77 53 B5
Lapwing. B77 53 E7
Launceston Clo. B77 52 B4
Lavender Rd. B77 52 C1
Lawrence Ct. B79 50 D3
Leedham Av. B77 51 G4
Leisure Wk. B77 53 D7
Leyland Rd. B77 52 C3
Liberty Rd. B77 53 D8
Libra Clo. B79 50 C2
Lichfield Rd. B79 50 A2
Lichfield St. B79 50 D4
Lilac Rd. B79 50 D1
Lincoln Av. B79 50 B3
Linden Clo. B77 52 D1
Lindera. B77 52 E1
Lindisfarne. B77 52 B3
Lintly. B77 53 F5
Little Church La. B79 51 E4
Littlecote. B79 50 B2
Litton. B77 53 F5
Lomita Clo. B77 53 B5
Lomond Clo. B79 50 C1
Longfellow Wk. B79 50 C1
Longfield Clo. B77 52 C1
Longlands Dri. B77 52 D2
Longleat. B79 50 B2
Lorton. B79 50 A2
Lothersdale. B77 53 F5
Lotus. B77 52 B3
Lovell. B79 50 C3
Lovers Wk. B78 50 D5
Lower Gungate. B79 51 E4
Lower Pk. B77 52 A4
Lud La. B79 50 D4
Ludgate. B79 50 D3
Lyndale. B77 53 D7
Lyneham Clo. B79 51 E1
Macgregor Cres. B77 52 D2
Macgregor Tithe. B79 51 E4
Madox Clo. B79 50 B1
Madrona. B77 52 F1
Magnolia. B77 52 E1
Magnus. B77 53 C7
Maitland. B77 52 D3
Malham Rd. B77 53 F5
Manor Rd. B77 52 A1
Mansfield Ct. B79 50 B3
Manston Vw. B79 51 F1
Manta Rd. B77 53 B7
Maple Rise. B77 52 E1
Mariner. B79 50 B2
Market St. B79 51 E4
Marlborough Way. B77 52 B4
Marlin. B77 53 B7
Marlow Rd. B77 51 G4
Marmion St. B79 51 E4
Marshall St. B77 51 G4
Masefield Dri. B79 50 D2
Masefield Rd. B79 50 D1
Meadow Pk. B79 50 C4
Meadow Rd. B78 50 C6
Meadow St. B77 51 F5
Meadowyrthe. B79 51 E2
Mealey. B77 52 C3
Medina. B77 52 C4
Medway. B77 52 B4
Melford. B79 50 B3
Mercia Clo. B79 50 B2
Mercian Pk. B77 52 E3
Mercian Way. B77 52 F1
Mercury Ct. B77 52 F2
Merganser. B77 53 E7
Metfield Clo. B79 51 F1
Mica Clo. B77 52 F3
Middle Entry. B79 51 E4
Mildenhall. B79 51 E1
Mill La. B79 51 E4
Milton Av. B79 50 D2
Minerva Clo. B77 51 G4
Monks Way. B77 52 D1
Moor La. B77 51 G4
Moor St. B79 50 D4
Moorgate. B79 50 D4
Morpeth. B77 53 A6

Mount Pleasant. B77 53 A5
Muirfield. B77 52 F1
Napier. B77 52 C3
Neander. B79 50 C3
Nemesia. B77 52 F2
Nevill St. B79 50 D4
Neville St. B77 52 B2
New Rd. B77 53 D7
New St, Glascote. B77 52 C2
New St, Mt Pleasant. B77 53 A5
Newstead. B79 50 B3
Nightingale. B77 53 E7
Ninefoot La. B77 53 C5
Ninian Way. B77 53 B8
Norman Clo. B79 50 C2
Norton Clo. B79 51 F2
Nymet. B77 53 C5
*Oak Tree Wk, Fontenaye Rd. B79 50 C2
Odham Clo. B77 51 F1
Offa Dri. B79 51 E4
Offa St. B79 51 E4
Old Cotton La. B79 50 B1
Old Hedging La. B77 53 B8
Oldbury Ct. B77 51 E3
Orchard Clo. B77 53 A8
Orchard St, Kettlebrook. B77 51 F6
Orchard St, Tamworth. B79 51 E4
Orkney Dri. B77 53 D6
Osbourne. B79 50 A2
Osprey. B77 53 E7
Ottery. B77 53 E8
Overwoods Rd. B77 53 D7
Oxbridge Way. B79 50 A3
Parbury. B77 53 B8
Park Farm Rd. B77 52 A4
Park Rd. B77 53 A8
Park St. B79 50 D4
Parkfield Av. B77 53 A5
Parkfield Clo. B77 53 A5
Parkfield Cres. B77 53 A5
Parkside. B77 53 C5
Parson St. B77 53 C6
Parsons Hollow. B77 53 C6
Pebble Clo. B77 52 F2
Peel Ho. B79 50 D4
Peelers Way. B78 51 F6
*Pegasus Wk, Bentley Way. B79 50 C2
Pembroke Clo. B79 50 B3
Pennine Way. B77 52 F4
Pennymoor Rd. B77 53 F6
Perrycrofts Cres. B79 51 F2
Pine Clo. B79 51 E1
Plantation La. B78 50 A6
Primley. B77 53 D8
Priory Clo. B79 50 D2
Prospect St. B79 50 D4
Pullman Clo. B77 52 E3
Purbrook. B77 53 C5
Queensway. B79 50 D1
Quince. B77 52 F2
Rainscar. B77 53 F6
Ravenstone. B77 53 F5
Raygill. B77 53 F5
Redhill Clo. B79 50 D2
Redlake. B77 53 C5
Redwell Clo. B77 51 G4
Redwing. B77 53 E7
Reedmace. B77 51 F6
Rene Rd. B77 51 G4
Ribblesdale. B77 53 F6
Richmond Clo. B79 50 D4
Ridgeway Rise. B77 52 E1
Ridgewood Rise. B77 52 E1
Ripley. B77 52 C3
River Dri. B78 50 D5
Riverfield Gro. B77 51 G4
Roach. B77 53 B7
Robert Clo. B79 50 C2
Robinson Clo. B79 50 B2
Roman Ct. B77 53 C6
Roman Way. B79 50 B2
Romney. B77 53 D5
Rosemary Rd. B77 52 C1
Rosewood Clo. B77 52 B1
Rosewood Ct. B77 52 B2
Rosy Cross. B79 51 E4
Rothay. B77 53 D5
Rufford. B79 50 B3
Rydal. B77 53 E6
Ryton. B77 53 D5
Saffron. B77 52 F2
St Andrews. B77 52 F2
St Austell Clo. B79 50 D3
St Christophers Dri. B77 52 A5

St Georges Way. B77 52 C2
St Ives Clo. B79 51 E3
St Margarets Rd. B79 51 E2
St Marys Way. B77 52 C1
St Peters Clo. B77 52 A4
Salters La. B79 51 E3
Sandpiper. B77 53 E8
Sandringham Ct. B79 51 E2
Sandstone Ct. B77 53 E6
Sandy Way. B77 52 E3
Saxon Clo. B77 53 D7
Saxon Mill La. B79 51 F4
Saxondrive. B77 51 F5
Scammerton. B77 53 E6
Scampton Way. B79 51 F1
School La. B77 53 A8
School St. B77 52 B2
Scimitar Clo. B79 50 B2
Scott Rd. B77 52 C1
Seaton. B77 53 D5
Sefton Rd. B77 53 B8
Selker Dri. B77 51 H4
Shakespeare Clo. B79 50 D3
Shannon. B77 53 D5
Shannons Mill. B79 50 D4
Sharpe St. B77 52 E1
Sheepcote La. B77 52 D2
Shelley Rd. B79 50 D2
Shelton St. B77 53 D6
Sherbrooke Av. B77 53 C7
Shetland Av. B77 53 D6
Shirley Wk. B79 50 C2
Signal Wk. B77 52 E3
Silica Rd. B77 52 F3
Silver Ct. B77 52 D3
Silver Link Rd. B77 52 C3
Silver St. B79 51 E4
Skidmore Av. B77 53 A8
Skipness. B77 51 H4
Skye Clo. B77 53 D6
Slingsby. B77 53 A6
Smithy La. B77 53 D6
Solway Clo. B79 50 D2
*Somerville Ct, Oxbridge Way. B79 50 B3
Sorbus. B77 52 F1
Sorrel. B77 52 F1
Spenser Av. B79 50 D3
Spinning School La. B79 51 E4
*Springfield Rd, Highcliffe Rd. B77 53 B5
Spruce. B77 52 F1
Standedge. B77 53 E6
Stanhope Ho. B79 50 D5
Steere Av. B79 51 E2
Stephenson Clo. B77 52 E3
Stevenson Rd. B79 50 D3
Stonehaven. B77 51 H4
Stonepit. B77 52 A4
Stoneydelph La. B77 53 E6
Stour. B77 53 E8
Stretton St. B77 52 C2
*Strode Ho Balfour. B79 50 D4
Sudeley. B77 53 A6
Summerfield Clo. B77 51 F5
Summerfield Rd. B77 52 B1
Sunbeam. B77 52 C3
Sunningdale. B77 52 F1
Sunset Clo. B79 50 D4
Swallowfield. B79 50 B3
Swanmote. B79 50 C4
Swift. B77 52 C3
Swindale. B77 53 F6
Sycamore. B77 53 C6
Sykesmoor. B77 53 F6
Talbot. B77 52 C3
Talland Av. B77 51 H4
Tamar Rd. B77 53 E8
Tame Ct. B79 50 D4
Tame Dri. B78 50 D4
Tame St. B77 51 F6
Tamworth Rd, Dosthill. B77 53 A8
Tamworth Rd, Glascote. B77 52 C1
Tamworth Rd, Kettlebrook. B77 52 A3
Tanhill. B77 53 F6
Tansy. B77 52 A3
Tarrant. B77 53 C5
Tavistock Clo. B79 51 F2
Teign. B77 53 E8
Telford Rd. B79 50 C1
Tempest St. B79 50 D4
Tennyson Av. B79 50 D3
Thackeray Dri. B79 50 D2
The Dell. B79 51 E3
*The Forge, Halford St. B79 50 D4

The Hedgerows. B77 53 D5
The Ridings. B77 51 H4
Thomas Guy Way. B78 50 C6
Thomas St. B77 52 B2
Thoresby. B79 50 B3
Thornby Av. B77 53 C5
Thurne. B77 53 C6
Thurso. B77 51 H4
Tilia Rd. B77 52 E1
Tinkers Green Rd. B77 53 D7
Tolman Dri. B77 52 A2
Tolson Clo. B77 53 A8
Torbay. B77 51 H4
Torc Av. B77 52 C2
Torridge. B77 53 E8
Torside. B77 53 F6
*Townsend Ho,
Balfour. B79 50 D5
Townwall Ct. B77 53 D7
Treasure Clo. B77 52 C1
Trefoil. B77 52 E1
Trinity Dri. B79 50 B3
Triumph. B77 52 C3
Trojan. B77 52 C3
Troon. B77 52 F2
Tudor Clo. B77 52 D2
Tudor Cres. B77 52 D2
Tutbury. B77 53 A6
Tutehill. B77 53 F6
Two Gates. B77 53 B6
Ullswater. B77 53 E6
Union Clo. B77 52 A3
Upper Gungate. B79 51 E3
Valley La. B77 53 C6
Vanguard. B77 53 B7
Ventura Park Rd. B78 50 C5
Victoria Rd. B79 51 E4
Wainrigg. B77 53 F6
Wansbeck. B77 53 C6
Wardle St. B79 50 D4
Warwick Rd. B77 52 C1
Watling St. B77 53 A5
Waveney. B77 53 C5
Welford Rd. B77 53 A8
Wellers Bourne. B79 51 E1
Wembury. B77 51 H4
Wenlock. B77 52 B2
Wesley Way. B77 52 C1
Wessenden. B77 53 F7
West St,
Kettlebrook. B77 51 F6
West St,
Tamworth. B79 51 F4
*Weymouth Ho,
Balfour. B79 50 D4
Whitesands Clo. B77 51 H4
Whiting. B77 53 B7
Whitley Av. B77 51 H3
Wigford Rd. B77 53 A8
Wigginton Rd. B79 51 E2
Willington Rd. B79 51 E2
Willoughby Rd. B79 50 C2
Wilnecote La. B77 52 A3
Winchester Rd. B78 50 C6
Windermere. B77 53 E6S
Windmill Clo. B79 50 D1
Windsor Clo. B79 51 F2
Witney Clo. B79 50 C2
Woburn. B77 51 G6
Wolseley. B77 52 C3
Woodcroft Av. B79 51 E3
Woodhouse La. B77 52 E1
Woodhurst Clo. B77 52 D1
Woodland Rd. B77 52 D3
Wordsworth Av. B79 50 D3
Wynyates. B79 50 B3
Wyvern. B77 52 C3
Yeovilton. B79 51 F1

UTTOXETER

Alexandra Cres. ST14 54 D3
Alleyne Pl. ST14 54 B2
Applewood Clo. ST14 54 C2
Ash Clo. ST14 54 C2
Ashbourne Rd. ST14 54 D1
Ashleigh Dri. ST14 54 A1
Avocet Clo. ST14 54 E4
Badgery Clo. ST14 54 C1
Back La. ST14 54 E3

Back Westlands Rd.
ST14 54 C4
Balance Hill. ST14 54 E4
Balance St. ST14 54 D3
Bank Clo. ST14 54 E4
Batemans Way. ST14 54 E2
Beech Clo. ST14 54 C3
Beechdale. ST14 54 C2
Benteley Rd. ST14 54 B2
Blackbird Clo. ST14 54 E4
Bradley St. ST14 54 E3
Brambling Clo. ST14 54 D4
Bramshall Rd. ST14 54 A3
Bridge Rd. ST14 54 F4
Bridge St. ST14 54 E3
Brookside Rd. ST14 54 E3
Bunting Clo. ST14 54 D4
Burton Ter. ST14 54 E2
Byrds Clo. ST14 54 B2
Byrds La. ST14 54 B2
Carter St. ST14 54 D3
Cedar Clo. ST14 54 C3
Chaffinch Dri. ST14 54 E4
Cheadle Rd. ST14 54 D2
Chestnut Dri. ST14 54 B2
Church St. ST14 54 E3
Clarkes Clo. ST14 54 E3
Cockstubbles Rd. ST14 54 D3
Collin St. ST14 54 D3
Colne Mt. ST14 54 D3
Copes Way. ST14 54 B1
Croft Gro. ST14 54 D2
Cross Rd. ST14 54 C2
Curlew Clo. ST14 54 D4
Davies Dri. ST14 54 B1
Derby Rd. ST14 54 E2
Dove Bank. ST14 54 E3
Dove Fields. ST14 54 F3
Dove Wk. ST14 54 F2
Eagle Clo. ST14 54 D4
Eastfields Rd. ST14 54 F2
Eaton St. ST14 54 E2
Elmwood Gro. ST14 54 B1
Fairfield Rd. ST14 54 D3
Fennel Clo. ST14 54 D4
Foxglove Av. ST14 54 D4
Gardner Pl. ST14 54 C1
Gas St. ST14 54 E2
George Elliot Clo. ST14 54 C1
Grange Rd. ST14 54 C1
Green Way. ST14 54 C1
Greenacres Dri. ST14 54 C1
Greenfield Dri. ST14 54 C3
Grenville Clo. ST14 54 B2
Hall Rd. ST14 54 C2
Hallam Rd. ST14 54 B2
Harvey Pl. ST14 54 C2
Hawthornden Av. ST14 54 B2
Hawthornden Clo. ST14 54 C2
Hawthornden Gdns.
ST14 54 B2
Hawthornden Manor.
ST14 54 C3
Heath Cross. ST14 54 C2
Heath Rd. ST14 54 C2
Heathfields. ST14 54 D3
Heaths Dri. ST14 54 D2
Heron Dri. ST14 54 D4
High St. ST14 54 D2
Highwood Rd. ST14 54 E4
Hill Clo. ST14 54 B2
Hockley Rd. ST14 54 D4
Holly Rd. ST14 54 C3
Howitt Cres. ST14 54 D1
Ivy Clo. ST14 54 C2
James St. ST14 54 D3
John St. ST14 54 D3
Johnson Rd. ST14 54 D1
Kestrel Clo. ST14 54 D4
Kimberley Dri. ST14 54 B1
Kingfisher Way. ST14 54 D4
Lambert Rd. ST14 54 B2
Lark Rise. ST14 54 D4
Leighton Clo. ST14 54 E4
Leighton Rd. ST14 54 E4
Lightfoot Rd. ST14 54 B2
Mallard Clo. ST14 54 D4
Manor Clo. ST14 54 C3
Manor Rd. ST14 54 D2
Market Pl. ST14 54 E3
Market St. ST14 54 E3
Marlborough Way.
ST14 54 B2

Mellor Rd. ST14 54 D2
Merlin Clo. ST14 54 E4
Milverton Dri. ST14 54 A2
Moor Gro. ST14 54 C2
Mosley Dri. ST14 54 C2
New Rd. ST14 54 B1
New St. ST14 54 D3
Northfield Clo. ST14 54 C1
Oak Clo. ST14 54 B2
Old Knotty Way. ST14 54 D4
Oldfield Rd. ST14 54 D3
Orchard Clo. ST14 54 C2
Park Av. ST14 54 D1
Park St. ST14 54 D1
Partridge Dri. ST14 54 E4
Parva Ct. ST14 54 B1
Pennycroft La. ST14 54 E2
Pennycroft Rd. ST14 54 B1
Picknall La. ST14 54 C3
Pine Wk. ST14 54 D2
Pinfold St. ST14 54 E3
Poplar Clo. ST14 54 B2
Primrose Way. ST14 54 D2
Princess Rd. ST14 54 E4
Queen St. ST14 54 E3
Redfern Rd. ST14 54 C1
Robin Clo. ST14 54 D4
Rosemary Dri. ST14 54 D4
St Marys Cres. ST14 54 D4
Sandpiper Cloi. ST14 54 D4
School Rd. ST14 54 B2
Shipton Clo. ST14 54 B2
Short St. ST14 54 D3
Silver St. ST14 54 E3
Skylark Clo. ST14 54 E4
Slade Fields. ST14 54 D2
Smithfield Rd. ST14 54 E4
South View. ST14 54 D3
Springfield Rd. ST14 54 D3
Stafford Rd. ST14 54 C4
Stanley Cres. ST14 54 C1
Station Rd. ST14 54 E3
Stone Rd. ST14 54 C3
Stoneyford Ter. ST14 54 E4
Summerfield Dri. ST14 54 C3
Sunnyside Rd. ST14 54 D2
Swallow Clo. ST14 54 D4
Swift Clo. ST14 54 D4
Sycamore Clo. ST14 54 B2
The Dove Way. ST14 54 D1
The Hollow. ST14 54 E4
The Hornbeams. ST14 54 C2
The Lawns. ST14 54 C1
The Meadows. ST14 54 C1
The Picknals. ST14 54 C3
Timber La. ST14 54 D4
Torrance Gro. ST14 54 B1
Town Meadows Way.
ST14 54 E3
Trinity Rd. ST14 54 E3
Tunnicliffe Way. ST14 54 A1
Uttoxeter By-Pass.
ST14 54 B1
Walkmill Clo. ST14 54 C1
Weaver Rd. ST14 54 C1
West Hill. ST14 54 E4
West Way. ST14 54 B2
Westlands Rd. ST14 54 D4
Westward Clo. ST14 54 D2
Windsor Rd. ST14 54 C2
Wood La. ST14 54 F4
Wood Leighton Gro.
ST14 54 E4
Wood Leighton Rd.
ST14 54 E4

WOMBOURNE

Apse Clo. WV5 55 C2
Banbery Dri. WV5 55 C4
Bankside. WV5 55 C2
Battlefield La. WV5 55 F2
Beggars Bush La. WV5 55 E3
Billy Buns La. WV5 55 E1
Birch Coppice. WV5 55 B3
Birch Hill Av. WV5 55 C3
Birch Hill Pl. WV5 55 C3
Blakely Heath Dri. WV5 55 D3
Bloomfield Clo. WV5 55 B3
Boss Gate Clo. WV5 55 C3
Botteham La. WV5 55 C4

Bramber Dri. WV5 55 D2
Bratch Common Rd.
WV5 55 C2
Bratch Hollow. WV5 55 D1
Bratch La. WV5 55 C1
Bratch Park. WV5 55 C1
Brickbridge La. WV5 55 B4
Bridge Clo. WV5 55 D2
Bridgewater Dri. WV5 55 D1
Bridgnorth Av. WV5 55 C4
Bridgnorth Rd. WV5 55 A3
Brindle Clo. WV5 55 B3
Brook Rd. WV5 55 C3
Brookside Clo. WV5 55 B3
Bull La. WV5 55 E1
Bullmeadow La. WV5 55 E1
Bumblehole Mdws.
WV5 55 C2
Bushwater Clo. WV5 55 D4
Calvin Clo. WV5 55 D4
Campion Clo. WV5 55 C2
Cannon Rd. WV5 55 D2
Carriers Fold. WV5 55 E2
Cedars Av. WV5 55 E3
Chapel Clo. WV5 55 A4
Chapel La. WV5 55 A4
Chapel St. WV5 55 A4
Chartwell Rd. WV5 55 C4
Chestnut. WV5 55 E4
Church Rd. WV5 55 A4
Church Rd. WV5 55 E2
Churchward Gro. WV5 55 D1
Churchwell Ct. WV5 55 E2
Clap Gate Clo. WV5 55 B3
Clap Gate Rd. WV5 55 C2
Clee View Rd. WV5 55 C4
Common Rd. WV5 55 D3
Copper Beech Dri.
WV5 55 E3
Corns Gro. WV5 55 C4
Crane Hollow. WV5 55 B3
Cranwell Green. WV5 55 D3
Dean Rd. WV5 55 C4
Deep Dales. WV5 55 B3
Dickenson Rd. WV5 55 D4
Dingle Rd. WV5 55 D3
Elder Gro. WV5 55 C3
Elm Tree Clo. WV5 55 D3
Foley Gro. WV5 55 B4
Forge Leys. WV5 55 B3
Forge Valley Way.
WV5 55 B3
Furnace Clo. WV5 55 B3
Gardeners Way. WV5 55 C4
Giggetty La. WV5 55 C2
Gilbert La. WV5 55 F2
Glendale. WV5 55 E3
Gravel Hill. WV5 55 E2
Green Acres. WV5 55 C4
Green Mdw Clo. WV5 55 B3
Greenfields Rd. WV5 55 D3
Greenhill. WV5 55 E3
Greenhill Ct. WV5 55 E3
Greenhill Gdns. WV5 55 E3
Greenlands. WV5 55 D2
Griffiths Dri. WV5 55 E4
Hatch Heath Clo. WV5 55 D2
Hawks Well Av. WV5 55 D3
Hazel Gro. WV5 55 E1
Heath House Dri. WV5 55 B3
Heath Mill Rd. WV5 55 B4
Heathlands. WV5 55 A3
High Meadows. WV5 55 E3
High St. WV5 55 E2
Highfields Dri. WV5 55 E3
Hill Side. WV5 55 B3
Holloway Dri. WV5 55 C3
Honeyborne Clo.
WV5 55 C3

INDUSTRIAL & RETAIL:
Heathmill Ind Est.
WV5 55 B4
Wombourne Enterprise
Park. WV5 55 A4
Jenks Rd. WV5 55 D3
Kirkstone Cres. WV5 55 D3
Ladywell Clo. WV5 55 D1
Lamb Cres. WV5 55 D3
Lanes Clo. WV5 55 B3
Lear Rd. WV5 55 E1
Lilac Clo. WV5 55 C2
Lindale Dri. WV5 55 C2
Link Rd. WV5 55 E1

Lockside. WV5 55 C
Longford Clo. WV5 55 F
Manor Gdns. WV5 55
Marlburn Way. WV5 55 E
Maypole Clo. WV5 55 E
Meadow La. WV5 55 E
Mill La. WV5 55 E
Millers Vale. WV5 55
Millfields Way. WV5 55 F
Millpool Clo. WV5 55
Moises Hall Rd. WV5 55 F
Monks Clo. WV5 55 C
Mount Clo. WV5 55 D
Mount Dri. WV5 55 D
Mount Pleasant Av.
WV5 55
Mount Rd. WV5 55 F
Neachless Av. WV5 55
Nursery Dri. WV5 55 G
Oaks Dri. WV5 55 E
Old Vicarage Clo. WV5 55 D
Ounsdale Cres. WV5 55
Ounsdale Rd. WV5 55 D
Park Av. WV5 55 G
Penleigh Gdns. WV5 55
Pinewood Clo. WV5 55
Planks La. WV5 55 A
Pool House Rd. WV5 55 F
Poplar Clo. WV5 55
Quendale. WV5 55
Redcliffe Dri. WV5 55
Redhill Av. WV5 55 D
Rees Dri. WV5 55 D
Rennison Dri. WV5 55 D
Richmond Gdns. WV5 55
Rookery Rise. WV5 55
Rookery Rd. WV5 55
Rosebury Gro. WV5 55
Rushford Av. WV5 55
St Benedicts Clo. WV5 55
St Brides Clo. WV5 55
Sandringham Rd. WV5 55
Sandy Mnt. WV5 55
School Rd. WV5 55
Smallbrook La. WV5 55
Smestow La. WV5 55
Station Rd. WV5 55
Stoney Brook Leys.
WV5 55
Stourbridge Rd. WV5 55
Sunny Hill Clo. WV5 55
Sunridge Av. WV5 55
Swinford Leys. WV5 55
Sytch La. WV5 55
The Broadway. WV5 55
The Celandines. WV5 55
The Croft. WV5 55
The Grange. WV5 55
The Hedges. WV5 55
The Longlands. WV5 55
*The Maltings,
Walk La. WV5 55
The Meadlands. WV5 55
The Paddock. WV5 55
The Shales. WV5 55
The Warings. WV5 55
The Willows. WV5 55 C
Trysull Rd. WV5 55
Uplands Dri. WV5 55 C4
Van Diemans Rd. WV5 55 D1
Victoria Dri. WV5 55 E2
Walk La. WV5 55
Waterdale. WV5 55 F2
Waverley Gdns. WV5 55 D2
Wedgwood Av. WV5 55 D4
Wesley Clo. WV5 55
Westbrook Way. WV5 55 D2
Westfield Dri. WV5 55 D2
Westleigh Dri. WV5 55 C4
Whites Wood. WV5 55 E3
Windmill Bank. WV5 55 E2
Windsor Rd. WV5 55 D3
Withymere La. WV5 55 F1
Woden Clo. WV5 55
Wombourne Pk. WV5 55 D4
Wombrook Dale. WV5 55 B3
Wood Rd. WV5 55 F1
Woodford La. WV5 55 A1
Woodford Way. WV5 55 B3
Woodhill Clo. WV5 55 D3
Woodhill Dri. WV5 55 D3
Woodlands Rd. WV5 55 E3